CAPTIVATE SALES COACHING

FOR REAL ESTATE AGENTS

MIKE ANDERSON
2ND EDITION
ISBN 978-1-66789-148-4
INTERCAP LENDING
© 2019-2023

CAPTIVATE
REAL ESTATE SALES COACHING

Residential real estate agents across the country are taking advantage of this powerful sales training program developed by Mike Anderson, a national sales coach, author, and CMO of Intercap Lending. Captivate will help you grow your business through a fresh approach to real estate marketing. You will learn how to leverage cutting-edge technologies like artificial intelligence, virtual reality, and today's digital marketing.

Captivate will also help you become a sought-after community expert drawing more buyers to your open houses, staging homes for top-dollar sales, and connecting homeowners with community influencers who become part of your referral partner network.

Send me your Captivate success stories and questions to captivate@intercaplending.com.

Mike Anderson
CMO, Intercap Lending

> "AGENTS THAT PROVIDE HOMEOWNER SUPPORT BEYOND THE TRANSACTION ARE IN HIGH DEMAND AND ARE MORE VALUABLE TO THEIR CLIENTS"

Mike Anderson

PREFACE
ABOUT THE AUTHOR

In 1995, about a year after our marriage, my wife and I bought our first place. It was a townhome in an older community a few minutes from where we attended college. I was applying to grad school and my wife had just started her career as a teacher. We decided it was a good investment even though we had no idea how long we would live there.

Six months later our whole world changed. My wife was expecting and I was offered a job on the other side of the country. The company that hired me was willing to pay for grad school and double our income, so we took it.

Fortunately, we managed to do some updates to the townhome during our short time there; things we already wanted to do for ourselves, that ended up adding extra value when we sold. To our amazement, our townhome went under contract the weekend it was listed. We walked away with $10,000 in net profit, which was a lot of money to us back then. That's when I caught the real estate bug.

I finished my master's degree and worked a nine-to-five for over twenty-five years. Along the way, we bought and sold dozens of homes, including several flips and rentals. Our experience may be unique, but nearly everyone has a history of where they've lived and some idea of what they would like to do next in real estate. For our clients, it's a lifetime cycle of buying, selling, refinancing, improving, and investing. According to the National Association of Realtors®, Americans move an average of seven times in their life. Sixty-five percent are homeowners. The other 35% rent from homeowners and investors.

Over the years, I've worked with real estate agents, brokers, builders, mortgage lenders, investors, title companies, property managers and even home warranty companies to help them build their sales and marketing strategies. What I learned is that it takes all of these professionals to help people navigate the needs and complexities of home ownership. And it's the real estate agent that's best positioned to organize this team

PREFACE
REAL ESTATE CONSULTING

of professionals into a real estate consulting offering for clients who are desperate to understand how to be successful property owners. The Captivate Program is the culmination of my 25-year journey in real estate consulting.

A **Real Estate Consultant** understands their clients' stories and continues to help them throughout their life as they buy and sell homes. If you have worked as a real estate agent for any length of time, you have likely consulted many of your clients beyond the basic transaction. Things like where they should buy, how equity works, and what makes a good investment. You've also referred them to lenders, accountants, and contractors. Now is the time to be more intentional about real estate consultations in order to separate your services from discount offerings that are narrowly focused on the transaction.

Good real estate consulting means you have useful knowledge and experience to offer your clients based on their distinctive needs. This may or may not be the case. No matter how good you are, it's nearly impossible to be an expert at everything that goes into buying, selling, and owning property, especially considering the uniqueness of each client and circumstance.

Many real estate agents work alone or on small teams that primarily support one another with the transaction. Real estate consultants build relationships with strategic partners that have expertise in lending, real estate law, accounting, home repair, home maintenance, interior design, property management, and other aspects of home ownership to better serve their clients. Your ability to bring these experts together into a client offering is what makes good real estate consulting. The intention isn't to hire these other professionals, but to support one another as each one brings value to your shared clients. You, as the real estate agent, are the tip of that sword.

Building a team of strategic partners and helping clients reach their aspirations of home ownership will captivate them for life. You will be amazed how easy it is to build your consultant-based real estate business, even if you are brand new to this industry.

PREFACE
REAL ESTATE SALES COACHING

The **Captivate Sales Program** includes several agent trainings that go along with this coaching workbook. You should attend these classes to better understand the underlying principles and overall Captivate strategy. You can view a calendar of upcoming Captivate classes at www.intercaplending.com/captivate. You can also join our Facebook group for recorded trainings and other resources at www.facebook.com/captivatesalescoaching

Participating Intercap Lending loan officers are trained as **Captivate Accountability Coaches** and can help you with your Captivate training and resources. Talk to your Intercap partner or find a loan officer near you by visiting www.intercaplending.com. You are not obligated to partner with Intercap Lending to take advantage of this training or its resources.

CAPTIVATE
Live classes and resources

Captivate Homeowner Lifecycle

The $20,000 Listing Presentation

Staging and Flipping

Digital Marketing: Video & Social Media

Grand Open House

Captivating Buyers

Community Go-to Agent

Time Blocking and Goal Setting

CONTENT

09 **HOMEOWNER LIFECYCLE**
CUSTOMER RELATIONSHIP MANAGEMENT

21 **$20K LISTING PRESENTATION**
THE MOST VALUABLE LISTING SERVICE IN YOUR MARKET

34 **STAGING AND FLIPPING**
HOMES THAT SHOW WELL, SELL WELL

43 **DIGITAL MARKETING**
TODAY'S REAL ESTATE SALES AND MARKETING

69 **GRAND OPEN HOUSE**
THE GRAND OPENING TO THE MARKET

85 **CAPTIVATING BUYERS**
BUYERS NEED MORE THAN A DOOR OPENER

101 **COMMUNITY GO-TO AGENT**
REAL ESTATE FARMING WITH VIDEO

115 **TIME BLOCKING POWER HOUR**
ONE HOUR A DAY TO DRAMATICALLY GROW YOUR BUSINESS

130 **THE MORNING ROUTINE**
CONTROL THE MORNING, CONTROL THE DAY

1

**INTRODUCTION
CAPTIVATE HOMEOWNER
LIFECYCLE**

CHAPTER ONE

CAPTIVATE'S HOMEOWNER LIFECYCLE

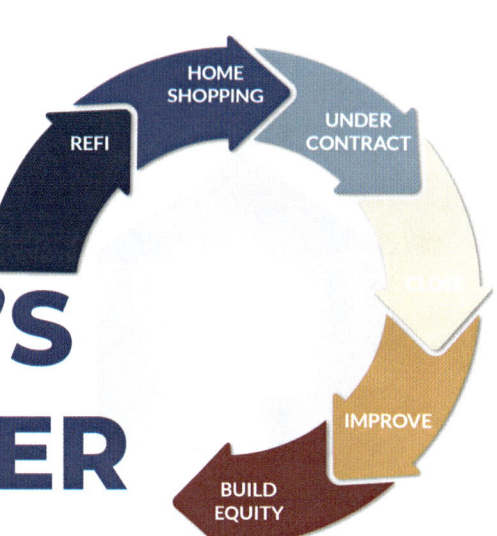

Captivate's Homeowner Lifecycle is a powerful new approach to lead generation and client relationship management for real estate agents. It teaches agents how to consistently capture new opportunities as people consider their next steps in real estate. Imagine helping renters prepare to buy their first place by the time their lease is up with a program called the **Pathway to Qualification**. Or helping a homeowner move up with a **Debt Consolidation and Home Transition Plan**.

> THE GOAL IS TO CREATE CLIENTS FOR LIFE. GENUINE RAVING FANS WHO ROUTINELY REFER YOU

The **Captivate Mission** is to create clients for life; genuine raving fans who routinely refer you. This may sound cliché, and it is if it's just wishful thinking. You can't create raving fans if you don't know how to exceed your clients' expectations. And you can't exceed their expectations if you don't know what they want when it comes to owning property. I'm not talking about what kind of property they want to buy, but why they want to buy and sell in the first place. What motivates them to consider real estate and what they care about before, during, and after the real estate transaction. If you can build your real estate offering around the transaction rather than starting and ending with it, your clients will keep coming back and routinely refer you to others.

Most real estate coaching and sales programs teach you how to stay top of mind with your clients and sphere of influence, how to make sales calls, how to ask for referrals, and how to self-promote so the people you know don't forget you're an agent. As good as these skills are, being a licensed agent gives you the right to assist in a transaction. It does not make you competitive. Growing your real estate business comes from defining and delivering how you stand out from other agents in your market (the area where you work).

I recently spoke with a guy who had just moved into our neighborhood. He mentioned that his brother-in-law is an agent, but he didn't use him. When I asked him why, he smirked and said, "I wanted to be able to fire my agent if I didn't like what he was doing, and I can't fire family," he then smiled and said, "And he's still mad at me."

As he shared more of his story, I found out he sold his old house with a discount service and bought his new home six months later with a different agent; one that he found on a popular real estate website while he was looking for homes. In the six months between the sale and purchase, he rented. He was openly exasperated by the whole experience and said he never wants to move again.

The most interesting part of his story is that he never mentioned what his brother-in-law could offer beyond the expected transaction. If the people you know can't tell the difference between what you offer from other agents, that's a problem. People who know you shouldn't choose your services simply because of the association. They should choose you because of your distinguishable value proposition—what you uniquely offer that helps your clients meet their goals. The three primary value propositions in real estate are:
1. Price (your commission)
2. Convenience (your availability)
3. Quality (your service before, during, and after the transaction)

The goal is to be the best at one of these value propositions and competitive at the other two. Most agents I meet want quality of service to be their primary value proposition. Discounting their commission and being available to show homes seven days a week, night and day, is not how they want to compete. But the distinction of their quality of service has to be real, or the client will opt for a better price or a quicker response.

Sellers are concerned about their net gain, so low commission attracts sellers. Buyers are anxious to get into the homes they find online, so an agent's availability attracts buyers. Marketing your quality of service can be tough in real estate. Yet agents who can help clients with a better overall experience are some of the most successful in their markets.

Some agents try to excel at all three of these value propositions to be ultra competitive, and customers will definitely take advantage of this if they can. The problem is this is hard to sustain, and it diminishes your brand. WalMart doesn't try to be Nordstroms, and BMW doesn't try to be Hyndai. If you want to grow in your market, you should try to be the very best at your chosen value proposition. If you want to be the best price, then own it. If you want to be the most convenient, then deliver convenience better than anyone in your area. If you want to be the agent with the highest quality service, then become the most captivating agent in your market when it comes to your service offering. The Captivate program can help you make "quality of service" your primary value proposition, and anyone who sees your work will have no doubt what makes you different.

Whether you are a veteran agent or brand new to this industry, Captivate can help you organize your systems and services into a high-value real estate consultant offering without having to reduce your commissions or be readily available every time someone calls.

CAPTIVATE'S
HOMEOWNER LIFECYCLE

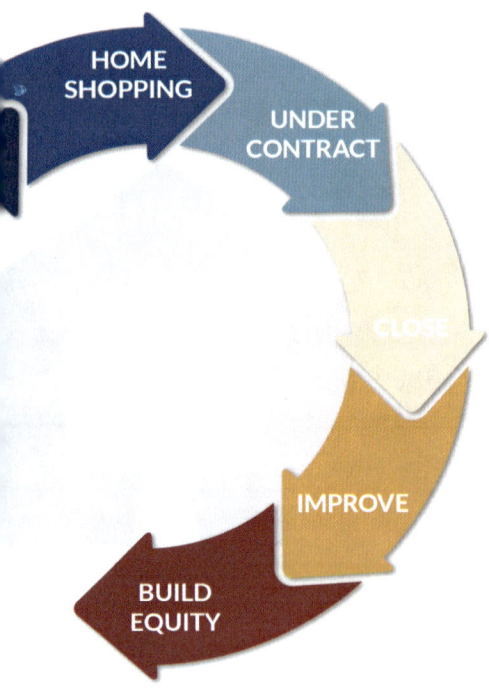

The **Captivate Homeowner Lifecycle** is a circle with six stages of home ownership. Each stage identifies what your client values at that moment in time. Providing meaningful value to clients at each stage of the lifecycle is how you create raving fans for life, which also gives clients a reason to refer you. Not simply because they like you, but because you gave them something they wanted beyond the expected real estate transaction. It's a circle because the buying cycle repeats throughout the client's life.

In contrast, a sales pipeline is linear. The typical real estate sales pipeline starts with a lead and hopefully ends with a closing. Many agents focus on managing their sales pipeline because that's where the money is, but there are a couple of problems with this approach.

1. Lead generation websites, discount brokerages, and many agents focus on capturing buyers who are ready to see a home. This happens during the last month or so of the **Home Shopping Stage** where competition is fierce, and convenience to open the door is the biggest differentiator.

2. Customers who do not engage with agents earlier in the buying process believe they do most of the work looking for homes and considering home values on their own using online resources. Do-it-yourself (DIY) is promoted as a cost-saving alternative to full-service commission, even by the very companies that sell leads to agents.

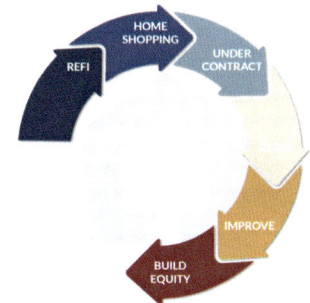

SIX STAGES OF THE CAPTIVATE
HOMEOWNER LIFECYCLE

The beauty of the Captivate Homeowner Lifecycle is you can capture leads at any stage of the lifecycle, even the less competitive stages. While other agents wait for a lead to click on a listing and request a showing, Captivate agents engage with their clients throughout the entire lifecycle. These high-value agents have a lot more to offer than opening a door and listing a home on the MLS. Clients rely on their Captivate agent before, during, and after the transaction and through all the years this is repeated.

1. THE HOME SHOPPING STAGE

Understanding each stage of the homeowner lifecycle is the first step to giving clients what they want beyond the expected transaction. It's about seeing the homeowner journey through their eyes. Exceeding expectations is where high-value agents stand out.

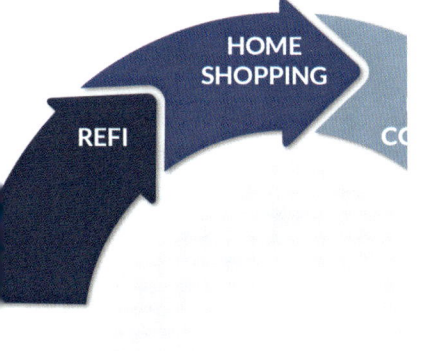

Since the Captivate Lifecycle is a circle, there's no start or ending stage as in a sales pipeline. I'm going to start with the Home Shopping stage since that's where most agents capture new leads, but capturing new leads can happen at any stage.

Our research found that today's home buyers spend a year or more considering a move, and the last three-to-five months of that year actively doing something about it, usually browsing online and deciding where they want to live. For many buyers, it's not until they want to get inside a home and make an offer that they contact a real estate agent for help.

THE AVERAGE HOME BUYER SPENDS A YEAR CONSIDERING A MOVE

During this year-long journey before an agent gets involved, home buyers consider things like affordability, out-of-pocket expenses, budget, the housing market, what kind of home they

15

©2023 All rights reserved. Confidential and Proprietary. Intercap Lending, Inc.

want, where the kids will go to school, and their commute to work. Unfortunately, they believe they need to figure this out on their own before they start shopping with an agent or speak to a mortgage lender.

Many of our clients struggle for years with misunderstandings about down payments, loan options, interest rates, equity, home maintenance, taxes, and many other considerations about owning property. Even current homeowners struggle with buying and selling in the same market, deciding if it's worth the move, total costs, preparing their home for a sale, becoming a landlord, and how to make a smooth transition without two mortgages or a place to live. Your ability to help buyers and sellers overcome their struggles and plan their next move is what real estate consulting is all about. And the demand for this is high because few offer it.

2. THE UNDER CONTRACT STAGE

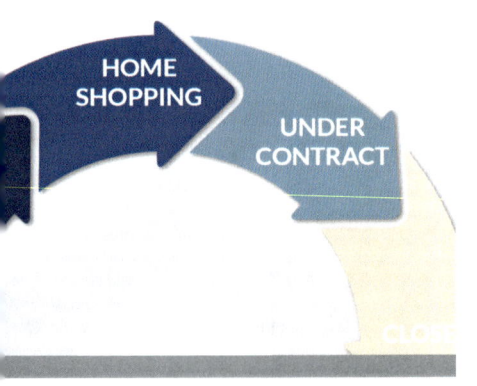

Everyone celebrates once an offer is accepted, at least for a day or two before the anxiety sets in. Will the loan go through? What's the inspector going to find? What unforeseen costs will pop up? What do we do if we don't close on time?

The Under Contract stage only lasts about four weeks, but it feels like an eternity to our clients. It's often the last thing they remember about you and their lender. The reason many people avoid moving is because it's an expensive pain in the butt. Many of our clients anticipate problems so they plan on temporary housing or paying two mortgages for a few months. Some wait until the pain of not moving is greater than the pain of the home transition nightmare.

Buying and selling shouldn't be such a hassle. There is a lot of opportunity here for agents and lenders to provide a better home transition service to their clients. Unfortunately, many agents are less engaged with their clients once an offer is

MORE PEOPLE WOULD BUY AND SELL IF THEY HAD BETTER SUPPORT

SIX STAGES OF THE CAPTIVATE
HOMEOWNER LIFECYCLE

accepted. The real work was getting them there. Some agents wait on the sidelines with their clients, hoping that the lender and escrow officer will get them to the finish line.

Captivate will teach you how to help your clients plan for a better transition and celebrate an on-time closing with regular progress updates. It takes planning and synchronized cooperation with agents, lenders, and Title to make this stage a successful closing to the transaction.

3 & 4. CLOSE & IMPROVE STAGES

While many agents celebrate their closings with a "Just Sold" postcard or a post on social media, the new homeowner is figuring out how to get their utilities set up, clean two homes and move, all on top of their normal day-to-day. Imagine all your belongings in boxes, not sleeping for days, eating fast food for a week, and being scared to look at your bank account. That's what moving is like for many of our clients.

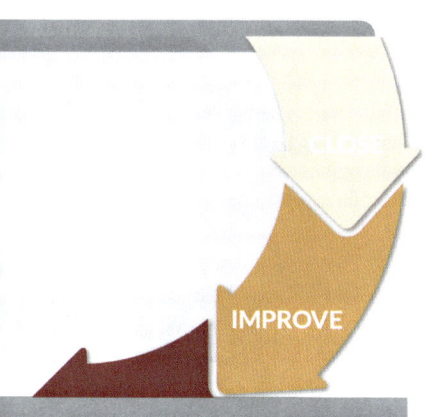

After new home buyers finally get settled in, they could use help getting their house in order. Some common new home buyer requests include:

- How do I maintain my new home systems and appliances like the water softener, water heater, furnace, A/C unit, sprinkler system, and fireplace?
- What kind of warranty or insurance do I have, and what does it cover?
- Are my smoke and carbon monoxide detectors working and up to date?
- How do I re-key my locks, reprogram my garage door opener, and setup security?

ON AVERAGE, HOME BUYERS HAVE 5 THINGS THEY WANT TO DO TO IMPROVE THEIR NEW HOME

- Where can I find a local handy man that can mount my TV's, install lighting and fans, and do a few other small updates?
- Where can I find a good local lawn care service?

On top of these more immediate needs, our research also found that new home buyers have an average of five home improvements they want to do within the first year of ownership. Painting, flooring, landscaping, and new furniture are usually at the top of the list. Agents are commonly asked for contractor recommendations. This is another opportunity to shine above agents and discount services who wait to be asked or don't have much to offer during these important closing and post-closing stages of home ownership.

Captivate can help you create a post-close service that will leave a lasting impression on your clients. This is yet another raving fan service that leads to more referrals and repeat business.

5. BUILD EQUITY STAGE

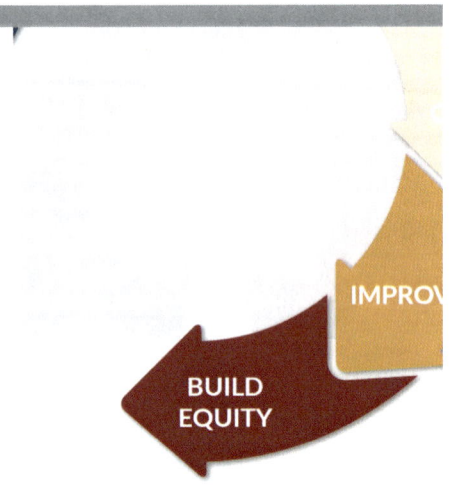

It could be months to years before your clients are ready to buy or sell again, but this doesn't mean they don't need your help. And it certainly doesn't mean there isn't ample opportunity to acquire new business. On the contrary, this may be the best time to capture new leads. While other agents wait until customers come to them during the last portion of the Home Shopping Stage, Captivate agents help people get ready to buy and sell during this time between transactions.

Beyond home maintenance reminders and contractor referrals, it's home equity that gets owners and first-time buyers thinking about their next step in home ownership. Your ability to engage them as they consider their next move is how you capture them as clients before other agents have a chance.

Home equity represents 87% of the average homeowner's net

SIX STAGES OF THE CAPTIVATE
HOMEOWNER LIFECYCLE

HOME EQUITY REPRESENTS 87% OF THE AVERAGE HOMEOWNER'S NET WORTH

worth. Potential equity is one of the top reasons people buy property. When your consultation services include helping people understand equity, you can tap into a larger pool of buyers and sellers who may want to make a move, but don't know how. In some cases, they don't realize they can. This is especially true with first-time buyers.

In partnership with **Homebot**[1], Captivate will help you give homeowners a monthly snapshot of their home's estimated value, equity position, and options for leveraging equity to pay down debt, refinance, and purchase more properties. This is a monthly home valuation and equity statement that comes from you to every homeowner in your SOI. It's so successful that we've seen a 78% month-over-month open rate and a 128% total open rate as homeowners revisit their digest several times a month. Homebot also sends a monthly digest to buyers to help them explore markets and understand homeowner costs and potential gain as opposed to renting.

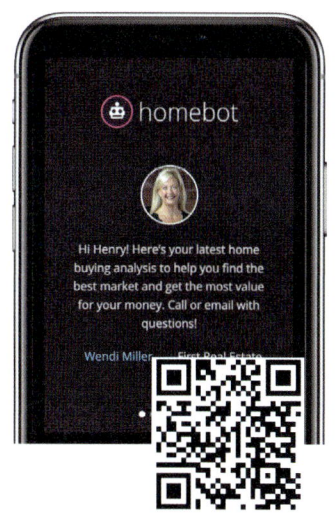

Captivate will teach you how to use technologies like Homebot to compliment your real estate expertise, not replace it. Determining a home's value requires an agent with a good understanding of the local market and each unique home in that market. We'll cover three points of a Home's **True Value** in Chapters 2 and 3.

6. REFINANCE STAGE

Before homeowners make their next move, many of them will refinance. They typically refinance to lower their monthly

---

1 "Homebot empowers consumers with personalized home finance insights and facilitates engagement with the experts than can help them manage this asset -- their loan officer and real estate agent."

19

©2023 All rights reserved. Confidential and Proprietary. Intercap Lending, Inc.

HELP CLIENTS TRACK THEIR EQUITY AND EXPLORE HOW TO LEVERAGE IT

payment or take out cash for a variety of reasons. Knowing when and why they refinance is important to understanding what your clients want as it relates to their finances and future home purchases. You want them to come to you for that lender referral. Your role as a Captivate agent is to be the first point-of-contact when it comes to everything related to real estate.

Another remarkable advancement of today's technology is the lender's ability to closely monitor a client's credit and debt. Some lenders, like Intercap Lending, assist clients with refinance and purchase opportunities based on automated triggers that help the lender know when a purchase or refinance is possible and in their client's best interest. Combine this with your monthly Homebot Statement and you can routinely assist your shared clients during this critical financial stage of home ownership.

One of my favorite examples is a married couple who was on the verge of divorce because of their financial struggles. An Intercap lender received a notice that the couple's home equity could be leveraged to pay off their debt and home much faster. The lender had no idea the couple was struggling. In the end, the couple was able to reduce their monthly debt payments considerably, with a plan to pay off their home and debt seven years sooner and with a lot less strain on their budget. This agent and loan officer consistently work together to help their shared clients with their financial goals. For them, it's not just about the next home purchase. It's about helping people navigate through this homeowner lifecycle with their real estate consultants as their trusted advisors.

These stages complete the circle of the **Captivate Homeowner Lifecycle**. Each stage is an important part of the homeowner journey that's repeated several times in your client's life. Providing support and value at each stage is how you create raving fans. The potential business growth is exponential as these fans share their experiences with the people they know.

SIX STAGES OF THE CAPTIVATE
HOMEOWNER LIFECYCLE

A CAPTIVATE MASTER CONNECTOR BUILDS A NETWORK OF BUYERS, SELLERS, PARTNERS, CONTRACTORS, AND COMMUNITY INFLUENCERS

With some effort, you will become what we call a **Captivate Master Connector**. As a Master Connector, Captivate will teach you how to build your network of buyers, sellers, partners, contractors, and community influencers. All these people need you as much as you need them to provide the best quality real estate service in your market.

The following chapters cover the **Captivate Real Estate Coaching Program** that converts an average agent into a Captivate Agent; a distinguishable high-quality agent in a sea of discount services and overworked agents.

2

$20,000 LISTING PRESENTATION

CHAPTER TWO

$20k Listing Presentation

MAKE YOUR LISTING SERVICE WORTH TALKING ABOUT

I call this the $20,000 Listing Presentation to remind me what clients pay to have an agent sell their home. In some cases, this is just a portion of the commission. The last time I spent $20,000 I expected something remarkable and exciting. Broker fees and commissions are not exciting, especially to the tune of tens of thousands of dollars. If referral business comes from clients who are happy about what they got for their money, let's get them more excited about a listing service that's worth the cost.

A great listing is the most visible way to showcase a high value offering in real estate. If done right, it includes magazine-quality pictures of a well-staged home and today's rich media technology:

- 3D Tours
- Drone Footage
- Video Home Shows

I'll also show you how to promote your listings with social media advertising and a **Grand Open House**, done with a level of detail and expertise only the best agents offer, but anyone can learn. This is **Captivate's $20,000 Listing Service**.

The consistent execution of knock-out listings is the absolute best marketing you can do for your real estate business. That's why Captivate starts with your listing services. We will review how to present and deliver a $20,000 listing service over the next few chapters of this book.

CAPTIVATE'S $20,000
LISTING PRESENTATION

3 ELEMENTS OF A WINNING PRESENTATION

1. Visual Presentation
The way you and your presentation materials visually reflect a $20,000 offering.

2. Oral Presentation
Your ability to listen, respond, and confidently communicate how well you can meet your client's goals.

3. Kinesthetic Presentation
The tangible evidence of your services. Leave-behinds that are professionally designed and written to help clients recall what you offer and how it stands out from competitors.

The **Captivate Listing Presentation** isn't a sales pitch. It's a commitment to excellence. Executing a quality listing is as important to your client's goals as it is to your brand and reputation. Any licensed agent can broker a sale. The best agents set themselves apart with remarkable listings.

The following listing presentation was created from homeowner and agent focus groups, and used in hundreds of successful listings. You may take any of these suggestions and add them to your existing presentation or use this presentation in its entirety. Either way, make sure the quality of your oral, visual, and kinesthetic or leave-behind elements of your listing presentation demonstrate a value that gets homes sold for more money, more quickly, and leaves a lasting impression of your high-value services. I recommend using a professional graphic designer to create your presentation materials, or use what we created.

You can download the PowerPoint slides and hand-outs from the Captivate Store at www.IntercapLending.com/Captivate

LISTING PRESENTATION MATERIALS

- Touch screen tablet or laptop with remote Internet
- Branded Home Shopping Bag and Folder
- Presentation slide deck and print outs
- Agent agreements (listing and buyer)
- Home Loan Consideration Sales Sheets

THE HOME TOUR

Before pitching your listing services, you need to learn more about the home and your seller's expectations. This helps to avoid the home value guessing game. The home tour is a listen and learning exercise. When you arrive at the home, and after introductions, say something like this:

"Do you mind if we take a tour of your home so I can get to know it better? My goal is to understand its **True Value**. Most agents rely on their Comparable Market Analysis (CMA) to understand a home's value. For me, that's just a baseline. I've already run a CMA, but before I come up with a final number, I want to consider your home's **Current Condition** and **Potential** for maximum value. I'm going to take some pictures with my phone as I tour your home, but don't worry, this is not for the listing. I'll have a professional take those pictures. These pictures are for me and my team to consider your home's true value."

As you tour the home and take pictures, ask the homeowner the questions listed below. Take notes and ask follow-up questions as needed. The goal is to get them to open up. This builds trust and helps you understand what the homeowner wants. The best agents win over their clients before they begin their presentation because they make it about the client and their home first.

- How long have you lived here?
- Why have you decided to sell?
- Where are you moving to and when do you hope to move?
- What do you like about your home?
- Is there anything that might need to be repaired?
- What do you think others will like about your home?
- What do you think should be done to help your home show it's best?
- What do you like about this area and community? (schools, parks, shopping, etc)
- What are you hoping for in terms of timing and net gain?

PAGE 1 PRINT
The brandable sales sheets are available in Total Expert. Ask an Intercap Loan Officer for a free copy of Total Expert.

Sign up for Total Expert

The first slide and printed sales sheet of the Captivate Listing Presentation serve as an infographic. This helps sellers recall your listing services more quickly. One of the biggest mistakes agents make with their presentation materials is to use too much text and poor graphics. Your presentation and leave-behinds should be easy for clients to review as they reflect the value of your $20,000-plus service.

Slide 1 Script
"My job is to help you get the most net gain for your home and sell it **just in time**, which means I'm going to do all I can to time the sale with your goals and next steps."

This is where you repeat their timing and net gain goals from the **Home Tour**. You are not committing to these goals. You are simply acknowledging what they hope for and what you can do to help them with your listing services.

"These images represent my primary listing services geared to optimize timing and net gain: **Verified Buyers, Staging, the Grand Open House, Video Marketing, and the 3D Home Tour.**"

VERIFIED BUYERS

I will help you attract more interested buyers

Not only will I generate more interest in your home, I can help you select the right buyer, manage negotiations, and monitor each step of the selling process for a smooth and timely closing.

PAGE 2 PRINT
Bring a copy of your state's purchase contract and highlight the areas where buyers specify anything to do with pricing and timing

Slide 2 Script

"My goal is to get as many buyers interested in your home as possible, even out of state buyers. This helps to drive up value and the urgency to buy. In a minute, I'll share how my advertising does this. **Verified Buyers** is what I do to make sure we pick the right buyer once offers come in. I want to ensure you have a smooth and timely closing, while generating the most net gain."

"My services include verifying the buyer's loan and funds, comparing competing offers, and negotiating with the buyer or buyer's agent for the desired sales price and terms."

"Here's what a purchase contract looks like. I've highlighted all the areas that buyers use to control their cost and timing. I'll make sure you understand all aspects of the offers you get and help you negotiate the one that works best for you."

27

©2023 All rights reserved. Confidential and Proprietary. Intercap Lending, Inc.

STAGE AND FLIP

Let me help you "flip" your home into a bigger profit

Most homes have some hidden value, and I can help you identify what you can do to maximize the return on your investment.

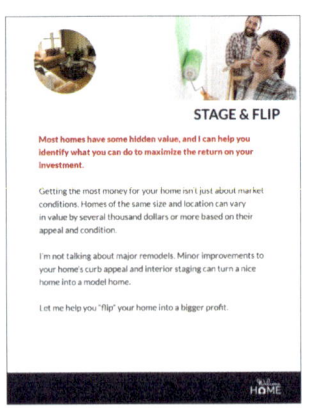

PAGE 3 PRINT

Slide 3 Script

"Homes that look their best sell faster and for more money. The way your home shows and how it's advertised are key to a quick and top-dollar sale, and I want to help you maximize your net gain."

"Once I am signed on as your listing agent, I will create a **Listing Report** that provides a recommended sales price and any suggestions to help you 'flip' your home into a bigger profit. I have a formula and an amazing team that will help to make this happen, considering your timing and net gain goals."

The next chapter is called **Staging and Flipping**. We will review the **Captivate Listing Report** and the four things every home needs to get ready to sell.

Your "team" consists of strategic partners like a stager and home service providers. Later in the book, I'll discuss how to build your team without any cost to you.

Homes that show well can sell for

5%-20% more.

USE THESE EXAMPLES UNTIL YOU HAVE YOUR OWN

Slide 4 Script
"Here are a few examples of how effective small improvements and staging can have on the value of a home, not to mention how much quicker it sells. In most cases, minor attention to details can make a significant difference in how the home shows and how much it sells for."

It's important to take the seller's home and situation into consideration when showing examples. If they plan to live in the home while it sells, focus on examples of staging homes with existing furniture. If empty, show the difference adding furniture to the main living areas can make. You can use these examples until you have your own. It's best not to give specific recommendations at this time. If they ask, let sellers know you will provide a **Listing Report** at your next meeting. Your goal at this point is to impress them with your approach to helping them maximize their home's value and have them sign your **Listing Agreement**. You do not have to give a suggested listing price before you get a listing agreement.

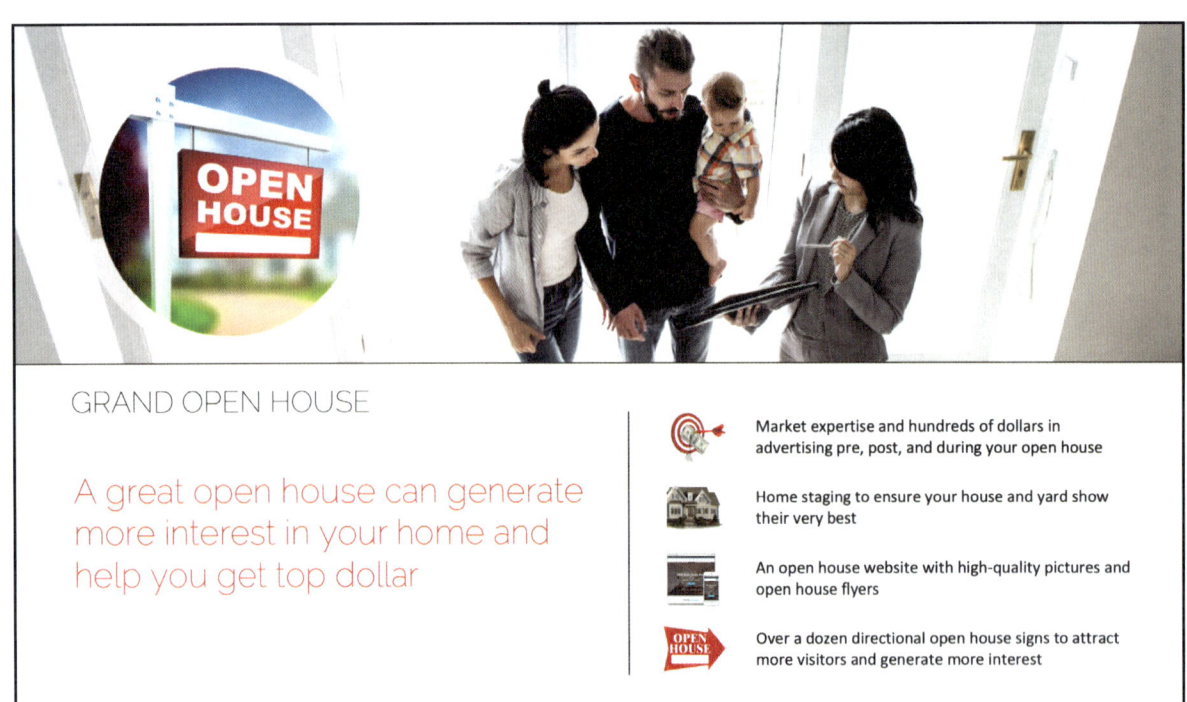

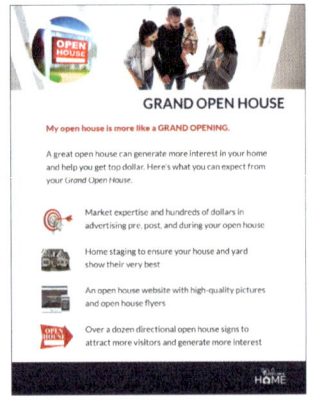

PAGE 4 PRINT

Slide 5 Script

"I don't host just any open house. An open house done right is its grand opening to the market. My goal is to get as many people interested in your home as possible and invite them to see it at its grand opening. This helps to drive more interest and urgency in purchasing your home the weekend it goes up for sale."

"I will spend hundreds of dollars advertising your home pre, post, and during your **Grand Open House**. I use drone, 3D tours, and professional photography. Not only will your home get promoted on the MLS to other agents and their buyers, I also advertise it on social media using artificial intelligence targeted marketing."

We will cover the **Captivate Listing Advertisements** in Chapter 4.

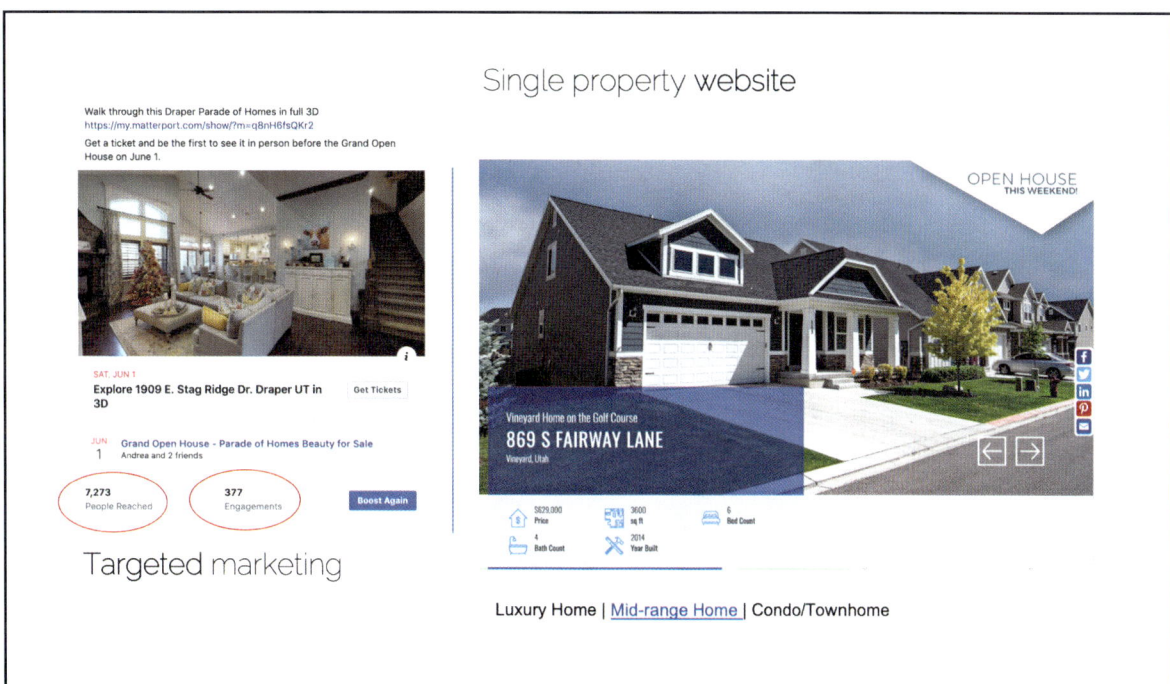

Single Property Website

Slide 6 Script

"Here's an example of one of the many ads I run to promote your house for the grand opening. Using AI-targeted marketing, I can attract buyers looking specifically in this area, even if they are house shopping from out-of-state. As you can see, I am able to reach and engage thousands of targeted buyers. I do five ads like this, so multiply these numbers by five to get an idea of the reach and engagement I generate. This advertising is on top of the standard MLS marketing every licensed agent offers."

"My advertisements include a **Single Property Website, Grand Open House Event Registration, Video Home Show, Drone Footage, and a 3D Tour.** Let me show you."

With your digital tablet and Internet access, show an example of a single property website. Use the example at www.homes.intercaplending.com/vineyard-6bed-home until you have your own. Flip through the large pictures and demonstrate how important professional, high-resolution photos are of a well-staged home. Scroll down to show the other features of this page, including the fact that no other homes are advertised.

Drone Footage

Video Home Show

Slide 7 Script

"Video is a powerful way to advertise real estate. I create two video advertisements for my listings: Drone and a **Video Home Show**. Drone footage helps to advertise the exterior of the house, yard, neighborhood, and community."

Play the drone video from the sample Single Property Website (SPW) or from one of your listings. As you play the video, talk about some of the benefits of their home exterior, yard, and community. If possible, try to have video examples of different price points and/or types of properties. For example, I have SPW examples with videos and 3d tours of a luxury home, mid-range home, townhome, and a condo. I'll use the example that is closest to the seller's property. Until you have all these, just use the sample provided. If you have an example of a **Video Home Show**, play this video next. You will learn more about the Video Home Show in chapter 5, page 75.

"In the Video Home Show, I film and discuss some of the main features of the home, and in most cases, invite a neighbor to talk about the benefits of living in this community."

32

©2023 All rights reserved. Confidential and Proprietary. Intercap Lending, Inc.

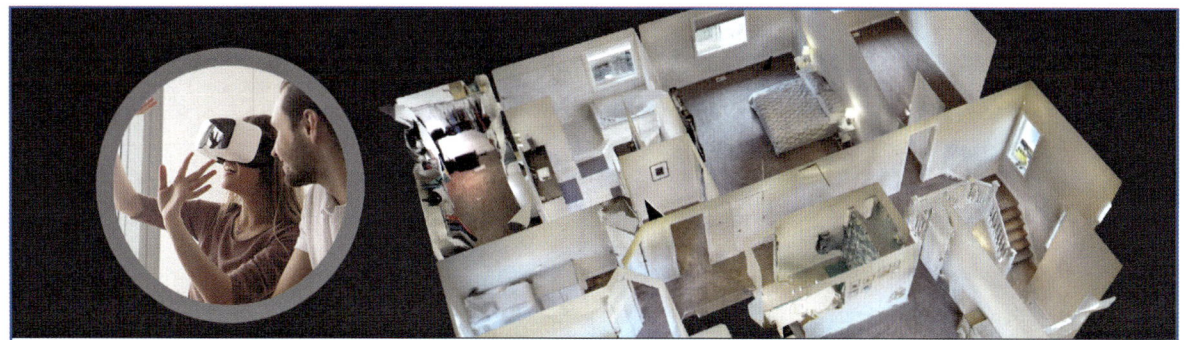

VIRTUAL TOUR

The future of home shopping is here today!

I will provide a 3D house scan and professional pictures to get your home in front of more people – *in its full glory.*

3D Tour Example

Floor Plans

Slide 8 Script
"Homes are three dimensional, so it only makes sense to advertise them in three dimensions. My service includes a complete 3D rendering of your home so potential buyers can virtually walk through your home as they do their online searches. Buyers spend a lot more time looking at homes with video and 3D Tours than without them. This media also makes it easier for buyers to revisit and share their favorite properties with friends and family."

Show an example of a 3D Tour. Use the sample provided until you have your own. Make sure to cover the following:
- Walk from room to room, looking up, down, and all around. Walk up and down stairs.
- View the floor plan and doll house views.
- Measure rooms, spaces, and furniture.

Bonus features that I always share are the **Matterport Floor Plans** and **Matterport Virtual Goggle View**. I bring a pair of Virtual Goggles and let them look at a home with the goggles.

SIGNED AGREEMENTS

After you complete your presentation, take a minute to share your leave-behinds. Your goal is to get a signed listing agreement. If the sellers are also going to look for a new home, have them sign a buyer's agreement and encourage them to get pre-qualified for a loan. Be confident that your services deserve an executed agreement before you get to work. If you don't believe your time and expertise are valuable, neither will they.

Once you are under contract, you can put together your **Listing Report**. This report will include the pictures you took during the **Home Tour** with recommendations for staging and improvements. You should give yourself at least a few days to put this together. We'll review these recommendations in the next chapter.

I don't recommend leaving a CMA after the presentation, especially without a signed agreement. It's all right to discuss the listing price during your presentation, but don't feel that you have to commit to a specific number until you complete your Listing Report. This way you are not backed into a price that you feel uncomfortable with. Sellers will respect that you take more effort to consider their home's True Value.

Download the listing presentation for free, and order the home shopping bag, presentation folder, and 3D Goggles here
www.intercaplending.com/captivate

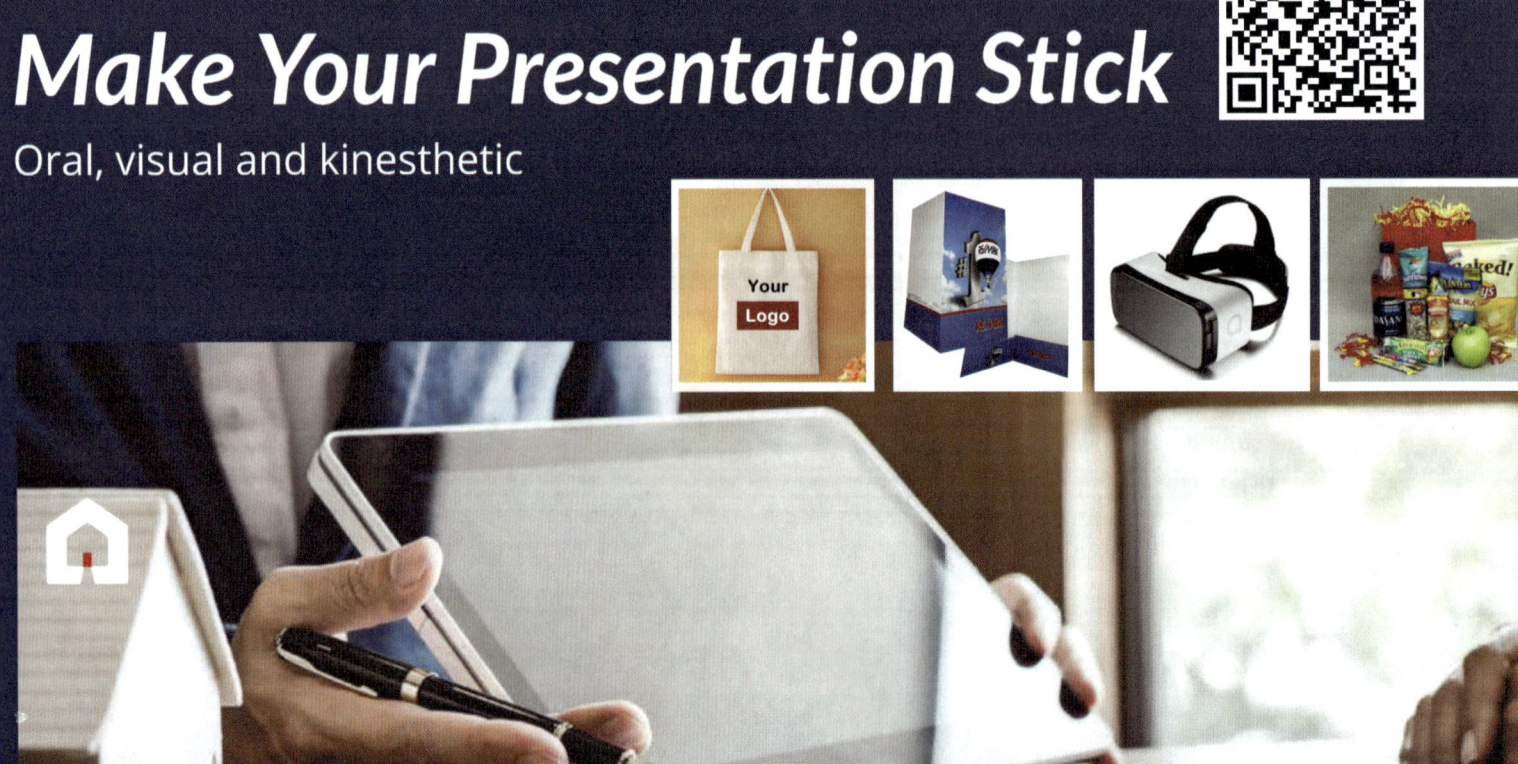

Make Your Presentation Stick
Oral, visual and kinesthetic

3

STAGING & FLIPPING

CHAPTER THREE
Stage & Flip

WE WANT TO LIVE IN BEAUTIFUL HOMES

Most homes are not ready to go on the market without some minor improvements. Your ability to prepare and sell beautiful homes will separate you from the average agent. Quality listings will generate more leads and help you build a strong reputation for high-value real estate services. In this chapter, we will review the four things every home needs before going on the market.

Your role as a real estate consultant is to help sellers maximize their investment with high-ROI improvement recommendations. It is not your responsibility to pay for home improvements or to do the work yourself, unless you offer this as a billable service.

Sellers may not be happy to put more time or money into the homes they are leaving, so it's your job to help them see the opportunity to make more money, hopefully much more. This is how you help your clients 'flip' their home into bigger profits. Your goals align with your sellers when their home sells quickly and for top dollar. Homes that show well, sell well.

1. CURB APPEAL

"Curb appeal can increase the value of a home 5 to 20 percent"
- John Gidding, HGTV Curb Appeal

CURB APPEAL IS FIRST THING BUYERS SEE

#1 CURB APPEAL - Buyers scroll through homes like a dating app, waiting to see something that catches their eye. The first thing they see online and as they drive up to the home is its curb appeal. If your listing's curb appeal is not very appealing, buyers are less excited about the home and sometimes don't consider it at all. You can't change the architecture, but every home can benefit from the following curb appeal updates:

Power Wash Exterior

HouseLogic by REALTORS® claims that washing a house can add $10,000 to $15,000 to the sales price of some homes. Washing the siding, brick, stone, eves, gutters, walkways, and driveway can make a dingy home look new again. I get my home power washed every quarter. Try it on your home, and don't forget to take before and after pictures. Make sure to hire a professional so you don't damage the home.

SPRING OR FALL CLEANUP

Trim Trees and Bushes

Overgrown trees and bushes can hide the house and make the home look neglected. I use a lawn care company to trim small trees and bushes. A tree trimming company is usually best for larger trees.

Improve Flower Beds

Adding fresh mulch and clearing out weeds and debris can make a huge difference in a home's curb appeal. Most lawn care companies offer a spring and fall cleanup that include lawn care, trimming, weeding, and flower bed improvements.

#1 CURB APPEAL

> "AS A REAL ESTATE AGENT, I HAVE FOUND THAT MOST HOMEBUYERS ARE MORE EXCITED ABOUT TOURING A HOME THAT LOOKS INVITING ON THE OUTSIDE THAN ONE THAT IS SAD AND DREARY, UNLESS THEY WERE FOCUSED ON BUYING A FIXER-UPPER."
>
> — JILL CHODOROV, ASSOCIATE BROKER

Green Manicured Lawn

Grass should be green and well-trimmed. Have your lawn care company use a nitrogen-rich fertilizer with daily watering. It can take a week or two to see a significant improvement. Dead grass may need to be replaced, and painting the grass is an option in some dryer climates.

STRATEGIC PARTNERS
You will need good lawn care and power washing companies for these services. We'll discuss your Strategic Partners later in this book.

2. CLEAN AND DEODORIZE
Most every home has a smell and the only one who can't smell it is the owner.

MOST HOMES HAVE A SMELL

#2 HOME ODORS - It's not rude to acknowledge that most homes have a smell. It's just the way it is. Not all smells are bad, but many people are sensitive to certain smells, and strong smells can turn potential buyers away or cause them to offer less money. Owners can't smell anything odd in their home because they are used to it. The goal is to have a clean home with little or no noticeable smells before it goes on the market.

Deodorizing a home means removing smells, not masking them with sprays, candles, or baked cookies. It's not the agent's job to clean or deodorize a home, and the owners shouldn't be asked to do the final clean because they can't smell the problems and likely won't do a deep clean. You will need a professional cleaner that knows how to deodorize. I had to teach my cleaners how to deodorize, and this is what I taught them:

Baking Soda
All carpet and fabric furniture get a light coating of baking soda. Let it sit for about 10 minutes and then vacuum. Make sure to do this before shampooing carpets. Throw out the vacuum bags before they get full so the smells don't escape. You can even add an open box of baking soda to a fridge. Baking soda is a remarkable deodorizer for a cheap price.

Coffee Grounds and White Vinegar
For stronger smells in bathrooms and laundry rooms, a bowl of fresh coffee grounds or white vinegar can pull smells out of the air. Make sure to empty or replace after a day or two, and don't leave the used coffee grounds inside the house. You can also try charcoal odor absorbing bags in smaller rooms.

CAPTIVATE'S
STAGING & FLIPPING

Avoid Dry P-traps

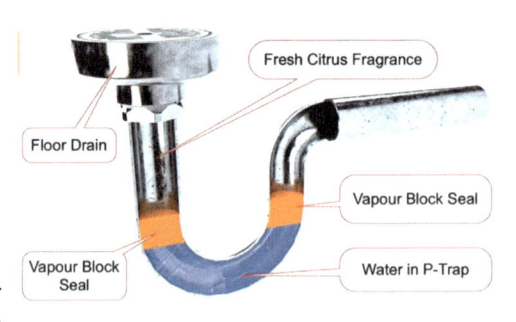

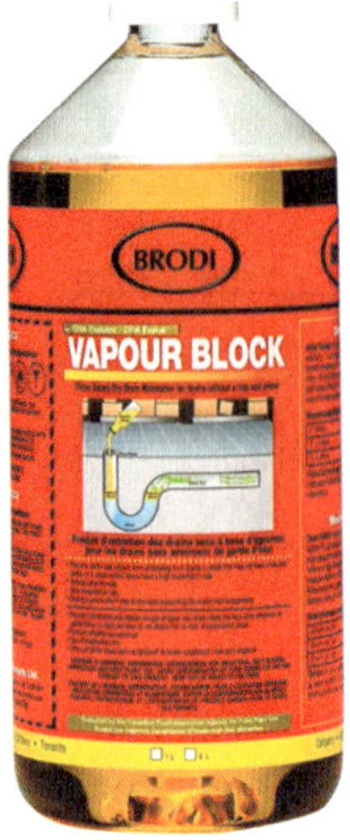

Every drain has a P-trap to keep the sewer smell from entering the house. This is simply a small water barrier that fills the U-shaped bend of the drain pipe. The P-trap can dry out in as little as a few weeks if water isn't going down the drain regularly. Empty homes and infrequently used drains need regular maintenance. For example, if your laundry room tends to smell, it may not be the dirty clothes, but the floor drain that never gets any water. Same goes for infrequently used bathrooms and floor drains in a garage or utility room.

If you don't want to regularly run water down these drains, you can also try the following:

- BRODI sells a product called **Vapour Block** that's made specifically for this problem. It's a little pricey at around $50 per bottle, but it lasts 3-4 months. Only add this to drains no one uses or it will get washed away.

- Another option is to add a 1/8 cup of olive or baby oil after you fill the P-trap with a bucket of water. The oil will sit on top of the water and keep it from evaporating as fast.

PERSISTENT ODORS

Really strong odors such as pet smells, urine, smoke, and mildew may require professional help from a home disaster company that specializes in remediation. They may use an ozone generator, KILZ, or other options that may require professional help. A persistent odor can significantly reduce the value of a home, so before you put a smelly home on the market, ask the client how much they are willing to lose in time and money if their home smells bad.

3. LIGHT AND DECLUTTER
Lots of natural light in an uncluttered home makes all the difference

LET IN THE NATURAL LIGHT

#3 DECLUTTER - It's a blessing to live with so much bounty, but this can also lead to having too much stuff in our homes. Most of us are pretty good at buying things, but not so good at letting them go. Many sellers don't realize how much stuff they have until they move. The last time I moved, I was convinced I needed a mid-sized moving truck. Once we started packing, I realized we could have filled two of the biggest trucks. We ended up selling and giving away a lot of stuff that year. If your sellers plan to stay in the house while it's up for sale, encourage them to start clearing it out and packing **before** listing the home because it will show better.

The following recommendations are for sellers that plan to live in the home while it's on the market:

Remove curtains and window treatments
Letting in natural light improves the pictures and showings. Curtains, blinds, and window treatments can also hold dust and smells. Removing window coverings lets the light in, and that's what you want. If blinds are worth keeping, open them up during the pictures and showings.

Pack and store extra belongings
It's best to have the sellers remove family pictures, knick-knacks, and other visible personal items. You also need to decide what furniture stays. Anything that doesn't stay should be packed and taken to a storage unit. Try to avoid having sellers use the garage, basement, or pod. Whether the sellers stay in the home or it's left empty, your job is to stage the home for buyers. It's no longer about the seller if they want top dollar.

CAPTIVATE STAGING

THE WAY WE LIVE IN HOMES AND THE WAY THEY SHOULD TO BE SHOWCASED FOR SALE IS DIFFERENT

#4 STAGING - Talking the seller into your Staging Plan

You will need to talk the seller into putting a lot of their items in storage, or completely emptying their home if no one will be living there. You also need to talk them into paying to clean and stage their home. Here's what to say:

"I want to help you get the most net gain for your home and sell it as quickly as possible once it's listed. Staging your home is the best return on investment advice I can offer. There's nothing wrong with the way we live in our homes, but the way they need to be showcased for sale is different. Let's make every picture look like your home came out of a magazine. As a bonus, your moving day will be much easier if a lot of your stuff is packed and ready to go."

Use before and after pictures to remind your clients how a staged home looks. Seeing is believing.

Professional stagers should be used for empty homes since they will provide the furniture, but you can learn how to stage homes with existing furniture. Either way, a stager is an important strategic partner. Once you build this relationship, your stager should be eager to help you consult your clients since they will also be their clients.

THE LISTING REPORT

The **Captivate Listing Report** provides recommendations for improvements and the suggested listing price or price range. Add the pictures taken during the **Home Tour** and include your **CMA report**. I like to show one picture from each area of the home with the key selling points and any recommendations. This **True Value** report helps you be more intentional about your listing price and sets you apart from other agents.

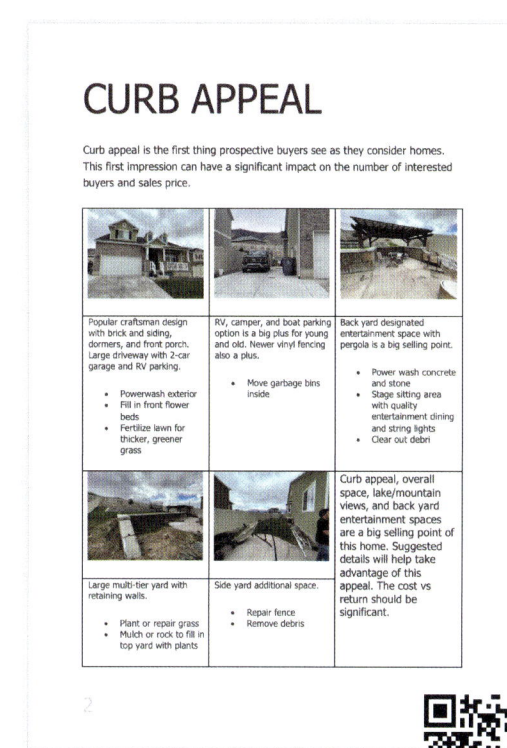

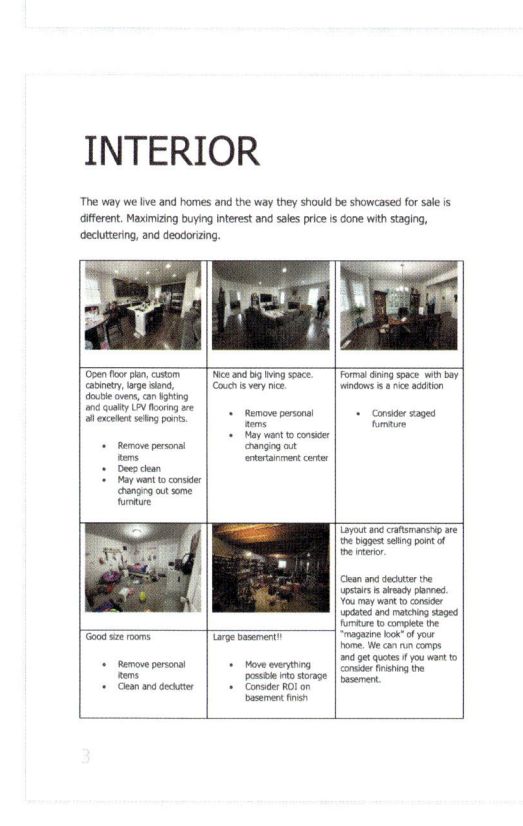

4

DIGITAL MARKETING

CHAPTER FOUR
Digital Marketing

EVERY GOOD AGENT IS A MARKETING PROFESSIONAL

To maintain the flow of the listing training from the previous chapters, I'm going to start this chapter with your listing advertisements. Towards the end of the chapter, I'll introduce you to another digital marketing recommendation for generating buyer leads through social media. In the next chapter, we'll jump back to the listing service with the **Grand Open House**, which also includes additional digital marketing training. At some level, digital marketing is included in every chapter of this book.

The truth is, nearly everything you do as a real estate agent can be enhanced by technology if you know how to use it. Two of the most valuable skills of a successful real estate agent are sales and marketing. Whether you are selling a home, selling your services, negotiating a contract, or managing your database, a lot of your success comes from your sales skills. Today's digital marketing can enhance your sales efforts by helping you extend your reach, increase engagement, tap into intelligent data, and deliver rich media content that today's customers expect when considering real estate.

Captivate takes real estate sales and digital marketing to a whole new level with the **Captivate Homeowner Lifecycle**. We've put the focus on the clients' needs during each stage of the lifecycle, giving them more of what they want, when they want it. In a sense, your best sales message is how you can serve your clients better than the competition no matter where they are in the lifecycle. Your business growth happens as you deliver these high-value services to clients who come back and routinely send you referrals. You will find that it's hard to compete if you don't take advantage of today's technology.

If you are a visual learner like me, I provided QR codes for examples and video tutorials. Use your camera phone to open these website links.

CAPTIVATE TECHNOLOGY WHEEL AND THE
HOMEOWNER LIFECYCLE

- HOME SHOPPING APP
- CRM OPPORTUNITY TRACKING
- HOME SHOPPING
- LOAN TRACKING APP
- UNDER CONTRACT
- REFI
- CREDIT & DEBT MONITORING
- CLOSE
- REVIEW MANAGEMENT
- IMPROVE
- SOCIAL MEDIA ADVERTISING
- BUILD EQUITY
- CONTRACTORS AND HOME MAINTENANCE REMINDERS
- MONTHLY HOME EQUITY STATEMENT

GOOD MARKETING IS GIVING THE RIGHT MESSAGE, TO THE RIGHT PERSON, AT THE RIGHT TIME. GOOD SALES IS DELIVERING EVERYTHING YOU PROMISE, AND A LITTLE BIT MORE.

SOCIAL MEDIA **ADVERTISING**

You are going to need **Facebook** and **Instagram business accounts** for this social media listing advertising. Use the QR links to the left for instructions on setting these up.

You cannot advertise on these platforms without their business accounts. You will not get enough reach or engagement unless you pay for it. One of the biggest misconceptions about social media is it's free to advertise and you need a lot of followers. These are for-profit companies that make their money from advertisers like us. Luckily, it doesn't take much money to reach the right people, and as your following grows, your money will go further. The real beauty of these social media platforms is their artificial intelligence targeted advertising based on user interests and behaviors. Follow this Captivate training and you will see an immediate impact on your ads and a long-term impact on your business, as long as you advertise regularly. Your listing advertisements on these platforms are the absolute best advertising you can do for your real estate business.

The Captivate Listing Advertisements consist of five ads placed on **Facebook** and **Instagram**. Although we won't cover this here, it also helps to post your listing ads on **LinkedIn** and upload the listing videos to **YouTube**.

You may feel overwhelmed the first time you go through these advertising steps. Here's the best advice I can give you:

1. If it was easy, everyone would do it and you wouldn't stand out. Neither would your advertisements.
2. The more you do it, the easier it gets.
3. If you do it right, your business will do so well you can hire a marketing assistant to help you. But you have to learn how to do it yourself first.

5 ADS OVER 5 DAYS

Your five social media listing ads will run for five days, leading up to your Grand Open House

LISTING AD FORMULA

1. MLS LISTING

2. PROPERTY WEBSITE LANDING PAGE

3. GRAND OPEN HOUSE EVENT LANDING PAGE

4. DRONE FOOTAGE

5. 3D TOUR

6. VIDEO HOME SHOW

The **Captivate Listing Advertising** is a formula you can use for every listing. The consistency of this advertising will help you sell your listings and remind all those who see your ads what they can expect when you help them buy and sell.

STEP 1 - MLS LISTING

Hopefully you were able to get your seller to follow your advice in your **Listing Report**. Cluttered or empty homes with poor curb appeal do not make for great ads. Try to schedule your pictures, drone, and 3D tour for the day your property is ready. Most of these media companies require you to schedule a week or so ahead of time, and they take a few days to get everything back to you. Timing home improvements, pictures, advertising, and your **Grand Open House** is an important part of your commitment to sell their home quickly.

Ideally, you will start advertising on a Tuesday for a Saturday Grand Open House. You and your seller may opt for a Sunday open house or multiple days. Both of these approaches work. We'll cover the Grand Open House in the next chapter.

You will want to create your MLS listing first, once you receive your listing pictures, video, and 3D tour. The order of your pictures and the description of the property are very important.

Listing Pictures
Every picture should get prospective buyers excited about your listing. Hallway bathrooms with the toilet as a focal point, messy closets, cluttered garages, and awkward room angles are not exciting, so leave them out. Buyers can look at the 3D tour or visit the property in person for a complete tour, and that's what you want.

PICTURES SET THE STAGE

The quality and order of your pictures can make a significant difference in how many buyers you attract.

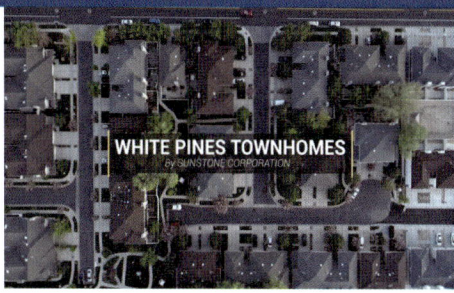

Start with a couple of the best pictures of the front of the property. I prefer the drone shots about 15 to 20 feet in the air. Next, add pictures of the inside of the property in the order of the best pictures. Don't worry about creating a walking path starting with a boring entryway when the home has a beautiful kitchen and master suite. Finish the lineup with the backyard and drone pictures of the community and amenities. This is more about quality than quantity. Your MLS listing is your first and most important ad.

Single Property Website
Visit www.homes.intercaplending.com/vineyard-6bed-home for an example

REAL ESTATE ADVERTISING

Property Description and Information

The property description helps buyers and their agents understand the important details of the property. Try to avoid too many superlatives. Let the pictures get buyers excited about how nice the property is and use the description to help them understand its key features. I like to start with any standout features, like views, swimming pool, 3-car garage, master on the main floor, penthouse, workshop, etc. Features that set the home apart from most properties. Then describe the property in the order of what buyers care most about. I start with the kitchen, master suite, garage, and entertainment spaces. Here's an example of a good property description.

Listing description example:

Move-in ready gourmet kitchen, 4-car garage on an oversized corner lot. Master on the main level with on-suite, jacuzzi tub, separate shower and walk-in closets. 6-burner gas range with walk-in pantry and granite counters. Open floor plan and vaulted ceilings with formal dining. Finished basement and entertainment room. Come to the Grand Open House this Saturday and be the first to see it in person! View the 3D tour and drone footage.

Fill out every field on the MLS before you go live. Don't leave anything for later. An incomplete listing frustrates buyers and agents. It can also get you in trouble for not knowing or verifying important details. Call the seller, your title rep, and the HOA for answers. Go to the property and measure rooms if needed. Although you will have a disclaimer about verifying square footage and the **Seller Property Description Disclosure**, there's no excuse for not knowing your property and publishing an incomplete listing.

SINGLE PROPERTY WEBSITE

STEP 2 - SINGLE PROPERTY WEBSITE (SPW)

Your SPW is one of the main **Landing Pages** of your social media listing advertisements. Each of the five ads will point to a landing page to help interested buyers get more information about the property and hopefully take the next step: Call for a showing, RSVP for the open house, or ask a question. A SPW makes a good landing page because there are no other properties to distract the visitor and it provides easy access to high-resolution pictures, drone video, and the 3D tour.

You can create these property websites in minutes with **Total Expert**, a free marketing and contact management system provided by Captivate and Intercap Lending. You can request a free license here: https://www.intercaplending.com/free-contact-management-system-for-re-agents/

Sign up for Total Expert

SINGLE PROPERTY WEBSITE
A unique listing landing page without showing other properties

Login to Total Expert. On the left navigation, select Web Marketing > Single Property Sites.

- Web Marketing
  - Single Property Sites
  - Social Media

At the top of the Single Property Sites page, click the blue CREATE button

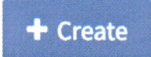

+ Create

Contact your Intercap loan officer or www.intercaplending.com/Captivate for more information and training on Total Expert and other Captivate Tools

SINGLE PROPERTY WEBSITE

SINGLE PROPERTY WEBSITE MENU
Options for building your site

Search by MLS#
Total Expert has the ability to download your listing from the MLS and create a SPW in seconds. This usually requires the listing to be live on the MLS for 48 hours, and the pictures that come from the MLS may be lower resolution. It doesn't take much to create a property website manually in Total Expert and the pictures will be better quality, so this is what I recommend.

Choose Your Template
My favorite templates are **Modern** and **Contemporary**.

Add Partners
Add yourself as the Agent Partner and add your Lender Partner so visitors can easily contact you for showings and ask your lender about mortgage loan options. This also adds your logo and contact information, making the web page compliant.

Help! Get video tutorials for a step-by-step guide

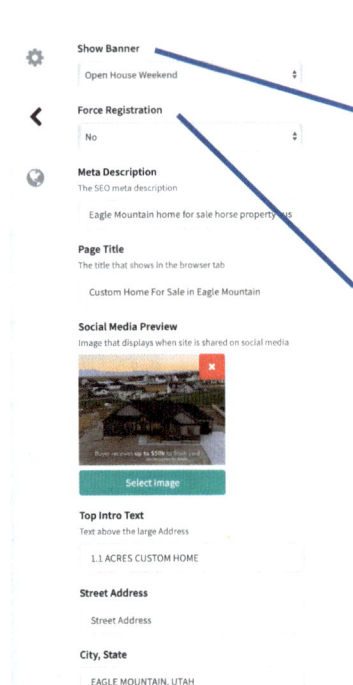

Edit Site (click on pencil icon)
You might be prompted to create a **Page Link Address**. This is the unique page name for the web. You can use any name that is not already taken. The name cannot have any spaces or special characters other than the dash. A good name is the street address or short description (i.e. lakeview-home-in-saratoga-springs).

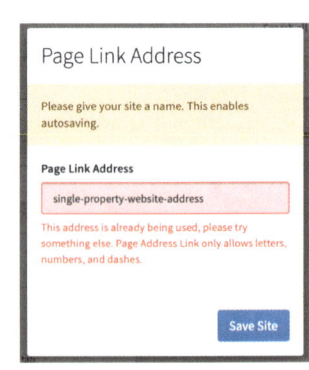

Show Banner
Display the **Open House Weekend** Banner for the upcoming Grand Open House. You can switch the banner as needed.

Force Registration
I do not recommend forcing registration. This requires the visitor to register before being allowed to see the page. It's a good thought, but this will turn away a lot of visitors who might otherwise get more interested after seeing the pictures, drone, and 3D tour. That's the primary goal of this landing page.

52

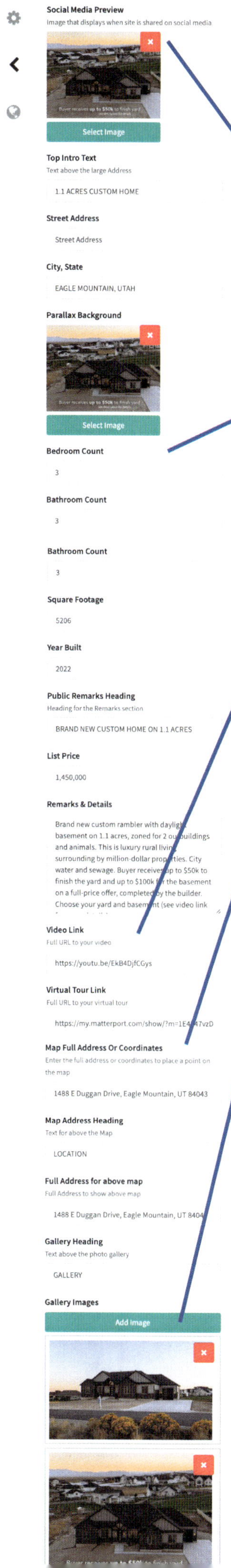

SINGLE PROPERTY **WEBSITE**

Social Media Preview
This is the image that will automatically display when you share your SPW on social media. Make sure to pick the best property picture. The Parallax Background is part of the website design. Pick your best property picture, inside or out and see how the web page updates on the right.

Property Information
Make sure all the property information is accurate. You can copy and paste the remarks and details from your MLS Listing if it doesn't automatically load. You should also include the MLS number in the remarks so agents can look up the property on the MLS.

Video and Virtual Tour Links
These web addresses will be provided by your photographer/videographer. Make sure to add these video and Matterport links to the MLS and your single property website.

Property Address
Make sure the property address is accurate and found on Google Maps. This provides a visual map on your site. You can check the address at https://google.com/maps.

Gallery Images
Add the same images in the same order as described in your MLS listing. You can move the order of the images on the left menu by dragging them. Images can't be more than 5MB each, so make sure your photographer knows these size limits. You can preview your site by clicking the **Preview** button.

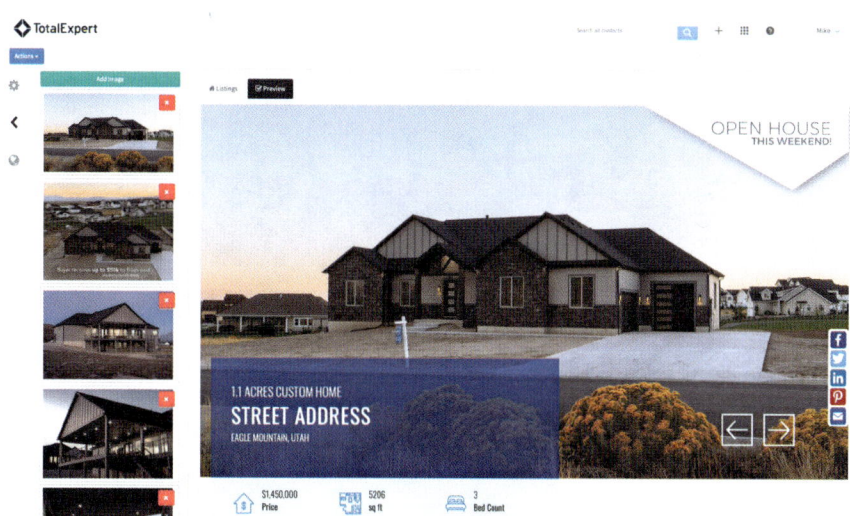

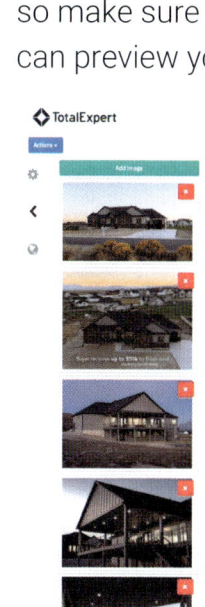

SINGLE PROPERTY WEBSITE

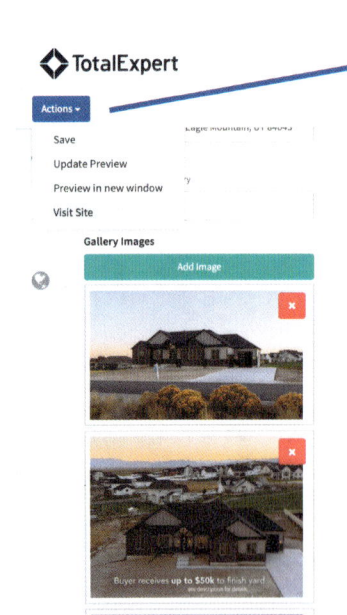

Save and Visit Site

Once you finish adding your pictures and filling out the form fields, click the blue **Actions** button on the top left of the page and select **Save**. Once saved, click **Actions** and select **Visit Site**. Note the web address in the top bar of your web browser. You will need this for your social media advertisements. You may want to copy and paste it somewhere so you don't have to search for it later. It should look something like https://homes.intercaplending.com/vineyard-6bed-home

Help!
Get video tutorials for a step-by-step guide

GRAND OPEN HOUSE
EVENT WEBSITE

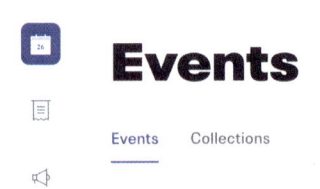

Step 3 - Grand Open House Event Landing Page

The second landing page is the open house event page. This allows buyers to RSVP for the **Grand Open House** and receive GPS directions and reminders. Most visitors will simply note the date, time, and address of the open house and show up. Some will RSVP to get a preview of the home thirty minutes before the open house. I'll explain this further in the next chapter. For now, let's review how to setup this event page using Eventbrite, which is free for this purpose.

GRAND OPEN HOUSE
EVENT WEBSITE

Create Event
Go to www.eventbrite.com and create a free account. Click the Create button for a new event.

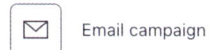

Basic Info
Create a title and add yourself as the Organizer. You will need to create an organizer bio. Next, add open house and real estate tags like the ones in the example. These hashtags cannot have spaces or special characters.

Location
Select Venue and add the exact address of the property.

Eventbrite.com

Basic Info
Name your event and tell event-goers why they should come. Add details that highlight what makes it unique.

Event Title*
Vineyard Grand Open House on Golf Course
40/75

Organizer
Mike Anderson

This profile describes a unique organizer and shows all of the events on one page. View Organizer Info

Tour | Home & Lifestyle | Home & Garden

Tags
Improve discoverability of your event by adding tags relevant to the subject matter.

Press Enter to add a tag
Add search keywords to your event
6/10 tags. 0/25

homeforsale × openhouse × openhouse2023 × openhouses ×
real_estate × realestate ×

Location
Help people in the area discover your event and let attendees know where to show up.

Venue | Online event | To be announced

Venue location
🔍 Search for a venue or address
Location is required.

Main Event Image
This is the first image attendees will see at the top of your listing.

- Recommended image size: 2160 x 1080px
- Maximum file size: 10MB
- Supported image files: JPEG or PNG

Main Event Image
Select the best picture of the house and add it as the main image. Then add a short summary like, "RSVP for a preview before the Grand Open House in [location description] and be the first to see it."

EVENTBRITE EVENTS

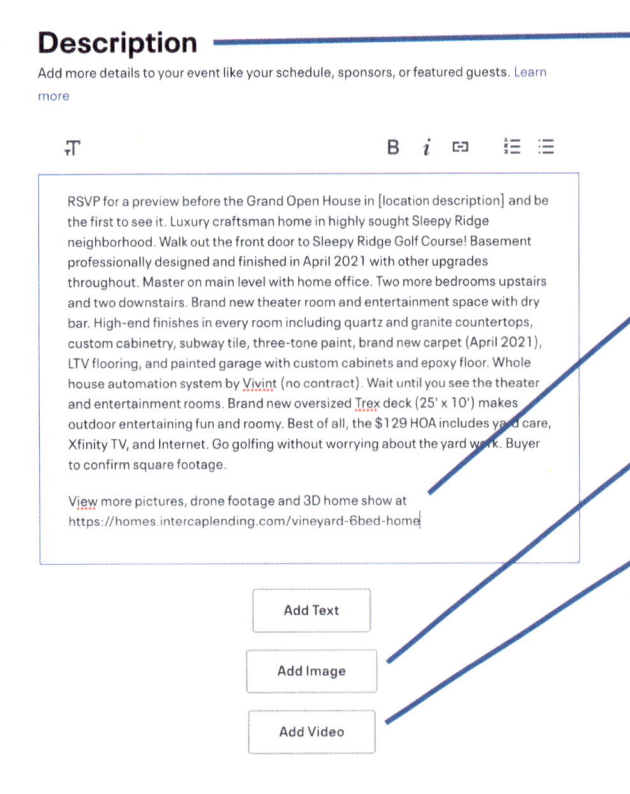

Description and Media
Copy and paste the description from the MLS. End the description with this call-to-action.

"View more pictures, drone footage and 3D home show at [single property web address]"

Next, add about five of the best images using the Add Image button. Add the drone video with the Add Video button. I recommend uploading your drone video to your YouTube Channel and then using the YouTube share link for Eventbrite. This helps with your search engine optimization (SEO) when people search your name or business on Google.

Add tickets and publish your event
Add free tickets with today as the sales start date, ending with the day and time of the Grand Open House.

Now you are ready to publish your event. Copy the web address of the published event and keep it with your SPW link. You'll need both of these links for your advertisements.

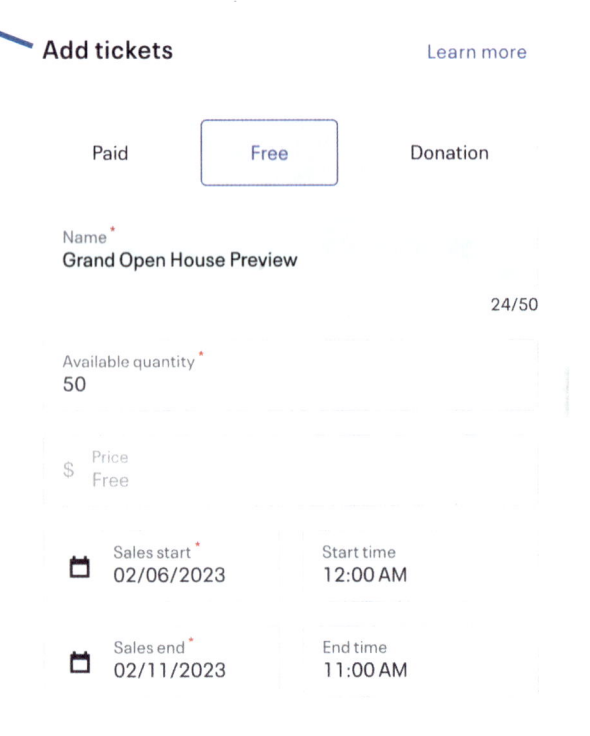

5 ADS OVER 5 DAYS
SOCIAL MEDIA LISTING ADS

STEP 4 - Five days of advertising until the Grand Open House

The most effective ads have a good hook and call-to-action, and follow the 2, 5, 15 second rule of advertising (explained below). Your ads should also create some urgency. You can follow this advertising formula with your five listing ads leading up to your **Grand Open House**. Here are the five listing ads:

1. Single Property Website
2. Eventbrite event and Facebook event (combined)
3. Drone
4. 3D tour
5. Video Home Show (see Chapter 5, page 73 for details)

For as little as $25 to $50 per ad, you can reach hundreds of buyers and agents currently looking for homes in the area. You will also remind your friends, clients, partners, social media followers, and many future clients of your real estate expertise with every listing you advertise. This advertising is for you as much as your listings.

Hook and Call-to-Action, and the 2,5,15-Second Rule of Advertising©

Your advertisements will not be very effective without a good hook and call-to-action. These help the viewer consider your offer and act quickly. A good ad should (1) capture the viewers' attention in two seconds, (2) communicate the hook in five seconds, and (3) help viewers take action within fifteen seconds or they will likely move on and forget your message. This is the 2, 5, 15-second rule of advertising combined with a good hook and call to action. Let's walk through what this means.

The 2-Second Rule

If your ad doesn't catch someone's attention in a couple of seconds, nothing else you do matters. You've already lost them. On social media, a video that automatically plays or an eye catching photo is key to the 2-second rule. For those considering real estate, the first thing a buyer should see is a beautiful home. This means your logo or headshot should be at the end of the video, not the beginning.

HOOK AND CALL TO ACTION

Every good ad has a hook and call-to-action, following the 2, 5, 15 Second Rule of Advertising© - Mike Anderson

The Hook and the 5-Second Rule

A hook defines, "What's in it for me?" It gives the viewer a reason to take a few more seconds to decide if what's offered is worth looking into. Otherwise, they move on. The great thing about social media advertising is you can specifically target home shoppers who are looking in the area, so you just need to catch their attention with a good hook.

The key to writing your hook is to find one or two top selling points of your listing that will lead buyers to want to learn more. In a sense, you are teasing prospects into wanting something so badly that they click a link, fill out a form, call a number, or send a text. What they do is the call-to-action. Why they do it comes from the hook.

For example, your listing may have dozens of selling points. If you list all of them in your ad, the viewer will likely give up before taking any action. Let's say one of the selling points of your listing is a nice kitchen. One of your listing ads could show a picture of the kitchen with the text, "Open House Saturday - gourmet kitchen with 6-burner gas stove and walk-in pantry (hook). Click to schedule a VIP showing before the open house (call-to-action)." This message will capture those interested in a nice kitchen and encourage them to act (click the link) in a few seconds.

The Call-to-Action and the 15-Second Rule

If the prospect can't figure out what to do once their interest is peaked by the hook, they'll move on. You usually have 15-seconds for the prospect to act on a good call-to-action. For example, let's say a home's selling feature is a 4-car garage and RV parking. Your ad may say, "Open house - 6bd, 4ba, 4-car garage with RV parking (hook). Call me for a showing at [phone number] or click image to schedule a preview before the Grand Open House (call-to-action)."

By creating five ads like this, you will give viewers more reasons and choices to consider your listing. The social media algorithms optimize this advertising formula wonderfully by showing more of your ads if someone shows an interest in one of them..

POSTING YOUR ADS TO
SOCIAL MEDIA

Help!
Get video tutorials for a step-by-step guide

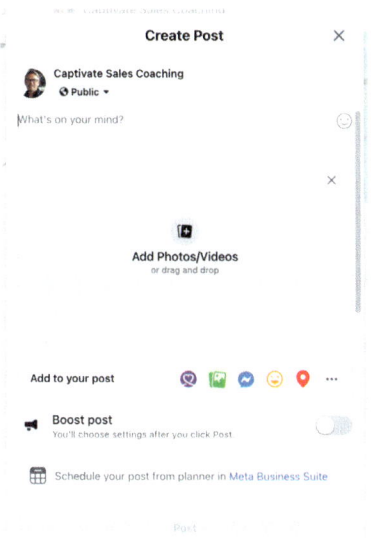

STEP 5 - POST FIRST, THEN ADVERTISE
Now that you understand the hook and call-to-action, you are ready to build your advertisements. Two of your five ads are videos: (1) Drone Video and (2) Video Home Show. The other three are website links: (3) 3D tour, (4) SPW, and (5) Eventbrite event. A bonus sixth ad is an image gallery of your property.

Posting Videos to Facebook and Instagram
You will want to upload your drone and **Video Home Show** videos directly to your Facebook and Instagram business accounts. Do not use a Vimeo or YouTube link in your Facebook or Instagram posts or the video will not auto-play.

You are going to create social media posts first, just like you've done many times. The only difference is you are going to use your hook and call-to-action in the comments. You should also do the following:

Use the **@** sign to tag people and **#** to hashtag

- Click the **Map Pin** icon to check in to the city or town where the property is located.
- Use the **Video Options** to add captions if your video has someone speaking, such as the Video Home Show video.
- **Tag** people that are in the video and tag partners involved with the sale, the sellers, your brokerage, etc.
- Add 5-10 **hashtags**, such as #openhouse

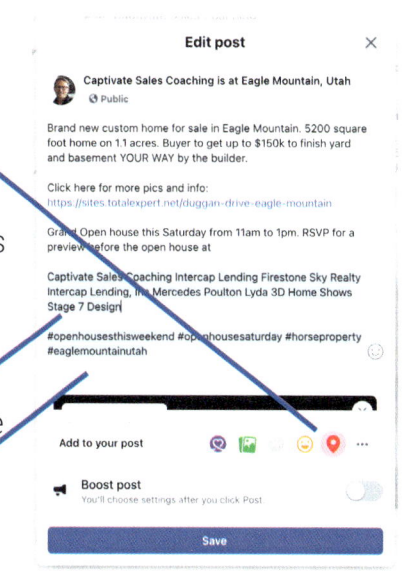

Due to the constant changes Meta makes to Facebook and Instagram, it's difficult to create a step-by-step guide for these post options that won't change in some way. The options will always be there. You may need to click around a bit to find them.

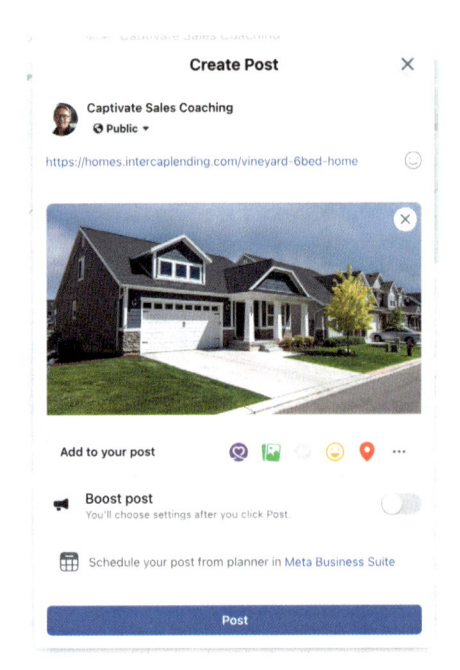

STEP 6 - POSTING WEB LINKS TO FACEBOOK

Your web link (URL) posts include the **SPW**, **3D tour** (Matterport) and the **Eventbrite event**. These URL posts only work with Facebook and LinkedIn. Instagram prefers photo or video over web links. You can add links to Instagram posts once you advertise. We'll cover that next.

Creating URL posts in Facebook are as easy as copying and pasting the URL into the post. Doing this automatically loads a picture from the web page with a title and short description, and makes the whole post clickable to the link that you pasted.

Once the image loads, you can delete the URL link and replace it with the hook, call-to-action, people tags, and hashtags. You should have five posts in Facebook and two in Instagram. The next step is to Boost them. Here's what the five posts in Facebook should look like.

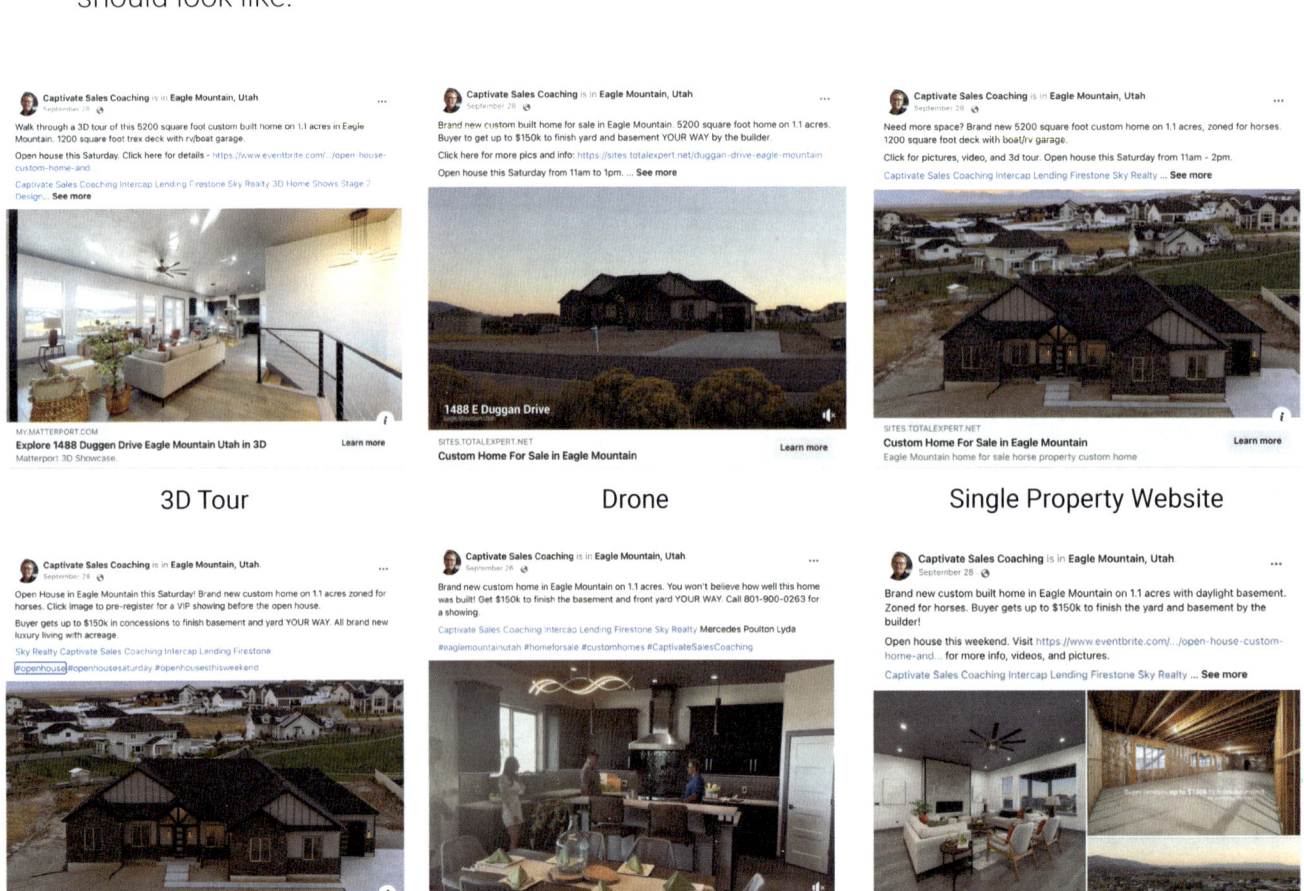

3D Tour

Drone

Single Property Website

Eventbrite Event

Video Home Show

Bonus Image Gallery

FACEBOOK & INSTAGRAM
BOOST

Help!
Get video tutorials for a step-by-step guide

STEP 7 - CONVERTING POSTS INTO ADS

There are a couple ways to advertise on Facebook and Instagram. The simplest way is to **Boost** a post. **Facebook Ad Manager** is an advanced option. If you know how to use Ad Manager, great, than use it. Make it a business development goal to learn how. Until then, boosting a post is as simple as clicking the blue **Boost post** button and selecting a few options. Here's what you need to know:

Boost Post
Click the **Boost post** button under each post to begin your advertising. The goal is to advertise for five days prior to the Grand Open House. For example, start all the ads on Tuesday for a Saturday Grand Open House.

Button
The button should point to the website link from the post, or one of the two landing pages if the post is a video or image. Your landing pages are the SPW and the Eventbrite event.

Special Ad Category
You MUST turn on the **Special Ad Category** and choose **Housing** for all real estate ads. If you don't, your ad will be rejected. This option follows the Equal Housing Opportunity Act regulations and puts some limitations on your target audience.

Meta may have changed the look or location of some of these options by the time your read this. Use the Help links for video tutorials (QR code on this page). I'll try to keep these tutorials updated with the changes Meta makes to its options.

INTERESTS & BEHAVIORS

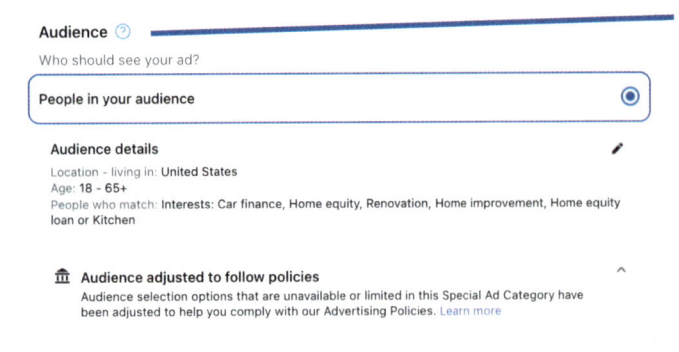

Audience
Facebook and Instagram have over 3.6 billion users world-wide as of Q2 2022. Meta collects everything their users do on their platforms and beyond. This is meta data of people's interests and behaviors. Couple this with artificial intelligent algorithms and Meta has a remarkably effective way to connect advertisers with likely customers because they know what interests them. Here's how you select your audience:

Audience Details
Click the pencil icon to edit the audience details. For the **Location**, type in the city or town where the listing is located with a 15 to 25-mile radius. This radius represents where buyers and agents are looking for properties.

Click the **Browse** link to see all your **Detailed Targeting** options. There are over a dozen interests and behaviors pertaining to real estate. Only select the ones that make sense for your listing. You can be a little picky with your selection. In other words, don't select every possible option that might represent a potential buyer. Otherwise, your ad will have a lower conversion rate.

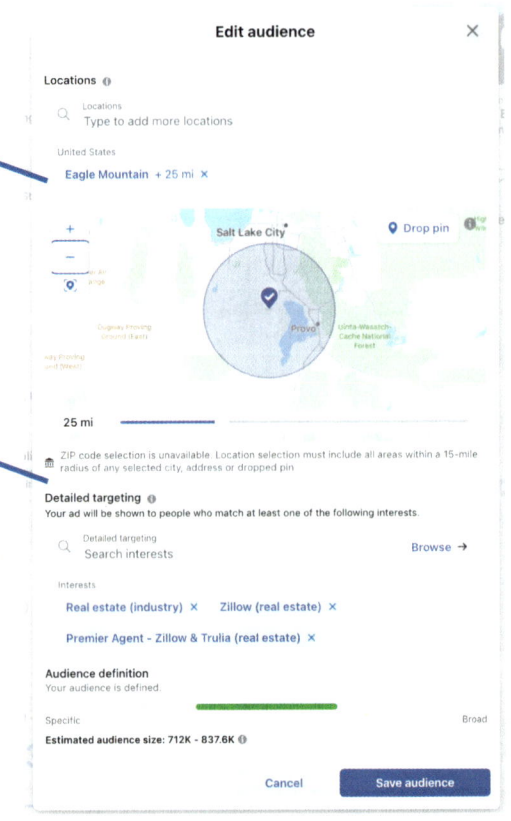

Duration and Budget
Select the number of days until your Grand Open House. It's not worth advertising less than a few days, so timing is important for this listing advertising leading up to the Grand Open House. I spend $25 to $100 per ad depending on the price of the house.

BETTER THAN
JUST SOLD POSTCARDS

Before and After Videos

We've covered your social media advertising leading up to the Grand Open House. In the next chapter, we'll talk about doing a **Facebook Live** and **Instagram video** during the open house. Once the house sells, I recommend you post a **Before and After** video to show what you did to get the property ready. Notice how much social media marketing you can do with your listings. Showcasing your listings and the efforts you take to sell beautiful homes is the best advertising you can do for your business. This is what future clients want to see.

For a **Before and After Video**, take the pictures from your **Home Tour** and compare them with the final listing pictures and video. Find the places with the biggest before-and-after improvements. Create a video that compares the pictures as you talk about how you helped your client get the most money for their home. Share this on your **Facebook Business Page** and boost it for another $50 to $100. Your best advertising is showing how good of a job you do for your clients. If you need some inspiration for these before and after videos, check out the video above, watch HGTV, and do a YouTube search.

I'll introduce you to **Camtasia** in chapter 7 if you need a video editor. Video is an important sales skill. If you are going to hire someone to help film and edit, make sure you are the actor and director. You need to be in your videos, but they should not be about you. They should be about the homes and people you work with. If you are still building your business, you can film, edit, and publish your own videos. It's easier than you think, and it's absolutely necessary in today's market.

SOCIAL MEDIA
LEAD GENERATION

Example of a Pro Agent Website

Pro Agent Website Offer

Facebook Group

Let's take a detour from your listing ads for a moment and talk about generating buyer leads with **Facebook Groups**. This recommendation requires you to have your own real estate website and a designated FARM (specific geographic area where you advertise your real estate services). I'll explain these two requirements and how they can help you generate buyer leads using a Facebook group.

Real Estate Website

Registered real estate agents have the right to host their own website that displays all the listings in their MLS. The licensed agent uses an IDX key (MLS website connection service) to display the MLS listings where the agent is associated. As a lead generator, the website shows the agent who owns the site as the person to contact for showings on every listing.

Captivate and Intercap Lending have partnered with **Pro Agent Websites** to offer a discount on their IDX agent website service. Pro Agent offers an IDX home search website with a buyer lead management system that's very affordable. Some of the many features include text and email listing alerts, search landing pages, video emails to clients, and blog pages, all hosted under your private domain (i.e. www.yourname-realestate.com). This agent website automatically displays and updates all the homes for sale in your MLS. You will need your own IDX-enabled website to do this social media advertising. Throughout this training, I'll mention several reasons why your own agent website is an important part of your technology stack to capture and manage new clients. Your agent website acts as your **Buyer Lead Management System (BLMS)**.

Visit www.proagentwebsites.com/intercap for more information

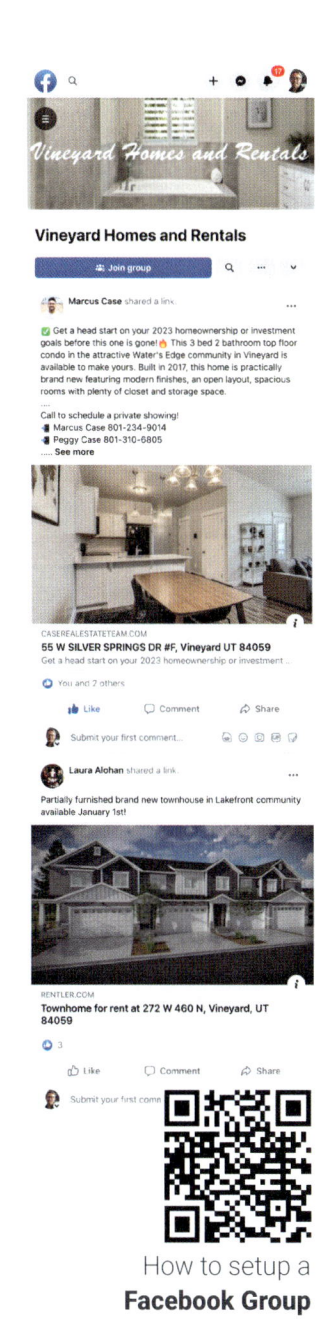

Real Estate Farming

Real estate farming is a marketing focus in a specific geographic area, like a small city. It can also be a focus on a niche buyer type, like first-time buyers. For this exercise, you will want to select a geographic farm where you will market all the homes for sale and rent in your farm. We will cover real estate farming in chapter 7, **Become the Community Go-to Agent**. You may want to wait until you finish chapter 7 before you pick your farm. For now, let's review the steps to capture new buyer leads from a Facebook group. You can come back later to follow these steps once you pick your farm.

Facebook Groups

The final piece of this farm marketing strategy is to setup a Facebook Group. Just as you setup a Facebook Business Page, you can also setup a Facebook Group (refer to the Facebook menu options or use the QR code at the bottom left of this page). A Facebook group is for special interests, clubs, and communities. Basically, anything people have in common and want to share as a group on Facebook. There are Facebook groups from cat lovers to neighborhood watch groups. The group I want you to setup is **Homes for Sale and Rent in [your farm]**. You can also set up a group for a niche farm like, **Investor properties for sale in [your area]**.

The best posts you should routinely put on social media to promote your services are homes for sale. A great way to do this is to share links to active listings from your agent website to this Facebook group, just as I showed you how to share your **SPW** on Facebook. Try it out. Copy a link from of any MLS listing and paste it in a Facebook post. It will automatically load the first image of the property and create a clickable link to that listing page. The key is to have it link back to you as a buyer agent. You can do this compliantly if you have an IDX website.

Having homes for sale show up routinely on Facebook is a great way to get buyers to consider properties they didn't

65

search for, as well as give people you know (or getting to know you) a friendly reminder that you are always on top of the local real estate market. Using a Facebook Group for these posts instead of your business page helps you focus on one specific area without appearing as if you only work in that area. It is also something you can do in a reasonable amount of time as opposed to posting listings from multiple cities. We'll discuss your daily routines in the last two chapters to ensure you spend the right amount of time doing the right things for your business growth.

Using your real estate website as the landing page for these Facebook posts ensures you are sharing these listings compliantly as a buyer's agent. Basically, you are helping buyers learn about the homes for sale in your farm area and pointing them to your agent website for more information and to request a showing.

It's important to understand that you are not advertising someone else's listing as your own. You are using a compliant, IDX agent website to share web page links to active listings. When it's not your listing, you are assisting the listing agent and brokerage as a buyer agent, sharing their listings to buyers you work with or hope to work with. The listing agent and brokerage manage the marketing of their listing through the MLS, which is reflected in the link to the agent website -- your website. You are simply copying and pasting the link into a Facebook post. If the listing changes to under contract or sold, the listing page is automatically updated to reflect this change. Any listing agent or brokerage that complains about buyer agents sharing links to a compliant listing page does not understand the nature of today's digital marketing, not to mention, how beneficial this effort is to help the listing agent. Agents should encourage this effort! It's not any different than the PPC advertising real estate lead services use to attract buyers to a listed home.

One of the smartest things about social media marketing is

their use of intelligent algorithms that understand how often people want to see your real estate posts. The more they are interested in real estate, the more of your posts they'll see. When they are not as interested, they see fewer posts. It's a brilliant way to throttle your marketing so you don't annoy your SOI on one end, while staying top of mind when they need you. In this case, you don't need to pay to advertise these Facebook Group posts. They work well organically. The combination of these Facebook group posts and your paid listing advertisements on your business pages makes a powerful social media marketing strategy for lead generation.

Here are the steps for posting to this Facebook Group
1. Create your Facebook Group, **Homes and Rentals in [your farm]**. Create a banner with a picture of a home or the community that gives the group title, without your head shot or logo. This isn't your business page. Invite your SOI to join the group, at least those that live in the area. In time, this group will grow organically. If needed, use Canva to create the banner.

Facebook Group Example

2. Each morning, do a search on your agent website for new listings in your farm. Copy and paste these links to your Facebook Group as a post. Write a hook and call-to-action, just like your listing ads. Pick one or two key selling points of the property as the hook. The call-to-action is to invite potential clients to call you for a showing. If you do this each morning, it should take twenty minutes or less to add all the new listings in your farm. Do this every day and you will become the real estate expert in your farm, virtually and literally.

3. Don't stop with the MLS litings. **For Sale by Owner (FSBO)** listings are also part of your farm, and this is an excellent way to capture FSBO sellers or help them find a buyer. Most FSBO listings can be found in your local classifieds or sites like

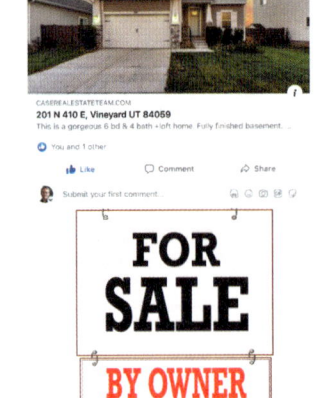

Craiglist. You probably know that FSBO sellers are not fond of agents who want a commission, otherwise they would have sold with an agent. That doesn't mean they won't pay some commission for bringing a buyer, and if their home sits on the market long enough, ask for help with selling. Here's how I suggest you approach FSBO sellers.

- Send a text that says, "Hi, I found your home for sale at [address]. I manage a Facebook Group with all the properties for sale and rent in this area. Would you like me to add your home? You can also add it yourself." Send a second text with the Facebook group web address. Send a third text that says, "I'm an agent, but I understand if you want to sell this on your own. Good luck!"

- You will likely get a response that could lead to helping them find a buyer or even help them sell. If you don't hear from them, wait a week and send this text: "Have you received an offer yet? You have a great place." See if they respond. If they do, don't be pushy. Let them warm up to your offer to help. Whether they have received offers or not, they likely need help. Make sure you don't compromise your brand or value proposition. You don't work for free or without a contract, and you are not a discount agent.

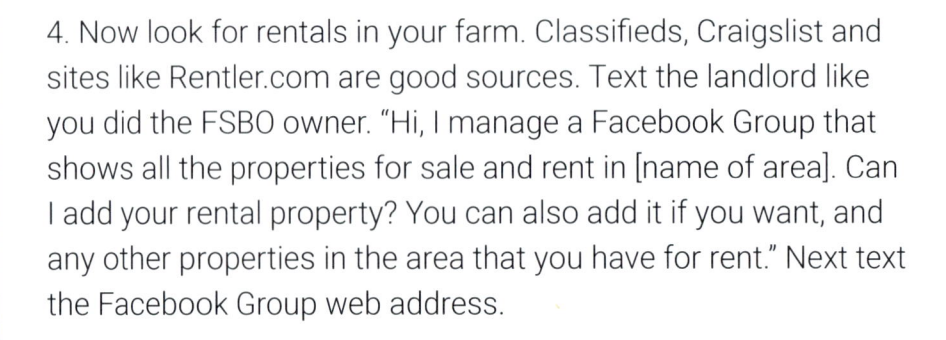

4. Now look for rentals in your farm. Classifieds, Craigslist and sites like Rentler.com are good sources. Text the landlord like you did the FSBO owner. "Hi, I manage a Facebook Group that shows all the properties for sale and rent in [name of area]. Can I add your rental property? You can also add it if you want, and any other properties in the area that you have for rent." Next text the Facebook Group web address.

Landlords and property managers make great partners, so take the time to get to know them. We'll cover working with partners in the last two chapters. We will also go over how to help renters get ready to purchase their first home with the **Pathway**

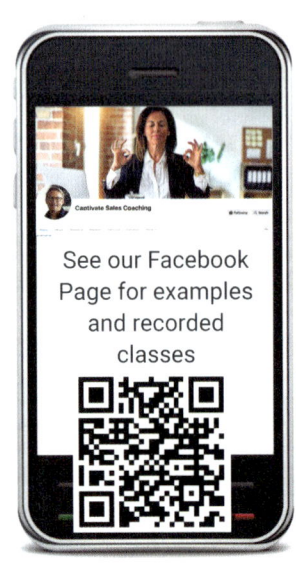

CAPTIVATE
Real Estate Digital Marketing

> IT'S TIME TO STOP TELLING YOURSELF THAT YOU CAN'T LEARN NEW TECHNOLOGY AND START SAYING, "I AM A MASTER OF MY CRAFT"

to Qualification program. Your Facebook group should provide a lot of opportunity to reach out to renters who respond to these rental posts.

In your Facebook Group settings, you can allow other people to post to your group, but set it so you have to approve their posts before they go live. That way you can control what's being posted. Once you've solidified a partnership with a property manager or investor, you can give them permission to post directly.

As I mentioned at the beginning of the chapter, digital marketing and technology are critical skills of a successful real estate consultant. Learn the technology to market, advertise, showcase listings, manage leads, and take care of clients through every stage of home ownership and your business will flourish.

| Help! Video Tutorials | Pro Agent Website Offer | Sign up for Total Expert | CAPTIVATE'S Technology Wheel |

5

GRAND OPEN HOUSE

CHAPTER FIVE
Grand Open House

THE BEST GRAND OPENING TO YOUR LOCAL HOUSING MARKET

Sellers believe a good open house will result in a quicker sale. Many listing agents think it's a waste of time. Both can be true. It all depends on how you approach the open house. Many agents don't take full advantage of this important listing service.

Done right, **Captivate's Grand Open House** is the culmination of a beautifully-staged home that's been professionally advertised to create excitement and urgency for its grand opening. Dozens or more anxious buyers come to a 2-hour event with open house signage that leads them through the neighborhood, into the house, and ready to make an offer.

If you haven't seen fifty, to well over one hundred people show up to an open house, you're not doing it right. Follow these Grand Open House recommendations and send your visitor count to captivate@intercaplending.com. The record is over two hundred visitors. I have personally been to Grand Open Houses with more than 150 visitors, so buckle up and get ready for the grand opening event your sellers and your real estate business have been waiting for. In this chapter we will cover the following:

- Getting the neighbors involved
- Open house signage and registration
- VIP tour before the open house
- Facebook Live
- Leaving a lasting impression on everyone who attends

I hope you can appreciate that every Captivate offering has a name, and every service has a process. Set procedures and consistent execution help clarify what you offer and what clients can expect when you are their agent. This is your brand identity.

As you grow, you can delegate responsibilities to marketing and transactional coordinators because you have established a clear process and expected outcomes. In business, we call these **Standard Operating Procedures (SOPs)**. Good businesses invest heavily in their SOPs because of how important they are to their operations, brand identity, and deliverables. The execution of your SOPs will directly impact your revenues and profit. At the end of this chapter, I will provide a **Listing Service Checklist** so you can refer to it every time you have a new listing. This is your listing SOP.

GRAND OPEN HOUSE PREPARATION

We already covered a good portion of your **Grand Open House** preparation in chapters 3 and 4. A great open house starts with attractive curb appeal, no odors, no clutter, and quality staging. The reason people come to your Grand Open House is because you spent hundreds of dollars advertising to those looking for homes in your area using AI targeted marketing. Your five ads provided hooks and calls-to-action with professional photographs, a 3D tour, drone footage, and landing pages that kept potential buyers engaged with your property for nearly a week. Some buyers will even take advantage of your VIP tour before the open house. Your ads also showcased how well you advertise your listings to help generate more leads.

The ad we haven't covered yet is the **Video Home Show**, which is a two-to-five minute teaser on the home staring you and

GRAND **OPEN HOUSE**

a neighbor. This is a video that you can film, edit, and publish yourself or with help from a marketing assistant. Anyone can learn how to do this, so please don't spend a lot of money hiring a professional videographer or film company. We provide step-by-step instructions in our live class, **Become the Community Go-to Agent**. There is also a **Video Publishing** tutorial in the **Help** section of our website and on our Facebook page. See links to the classes and help videos to the left. Chapter 7 also provides help with your video production.

Creating and publishing videos is an important skill of a Captivate agent. These videos help sell your homes and promote your business. The intuitive, drag-and-drop interface of today's video technology makes video production easy, so don't let it intimidate you. You already have a high-quality video camera in your smart phone. I'll show you how to use it.

VIDEO HOME SHOW

The **Video Home Show** has two parts: The **Home Teaser** and the **Neighbor Interview**. The Home Teaser is a two-to-three-minute teaser about the top property features. You can take the hooks from your listing ads and make a short video of these primary selling points. Here's what you need to make your video:

- Smart phone with video camera
- 6' tripod with a phone attachment
- Lav mic or hand mic that plugs into your phone
- Phone stabilizer (optional)

Tripod with Smartphone Mount

Captivate Store

Dual Microphone Kit

73

©2023 All rights reserved. Confidential and Proprietary. Intercap Lending, Inc.

GRAND **OPEN HOUSE**

Video Home Show instructions

Place your tripod with your phone at eye level in the kitchen or another nice area of the home to serve as a backdrop for your video. You are going to stand in one place and talk about the top selling points of the home without walking around. Connect a microphone to your phone so the sound is clear. This video is just a teaser, so don't worry about covering every selling point or doing a complete home tour. Your goal is to get buyers to come to the house, so a few of the top selling points are enough.

After you finish your teaser, film some video sweeps of the areas of the home that you spoke about. We call this B-roll. You are going to lay this B-roll over the video of you talking about these home features. Use a stabilizer or slow and smooth sweeps to film this B-roll video. Again, you don't have to show every room. The teaser should only be a few minutes long unless you feel more time is needed or you become really good at these videos. See some examples on the following page.

NEIGHBOR INTERVIEW

Next, you are going to visit neighbors and ask them what they love about living in the neighborhood, and if willing, get them to share this on your video. I like to ask my sellers if they have a neighbor friend who would be willing to talk with us. This is also a great way to get to know the neighbors and invite them to the Grand Open House.

Here's what I say to neighbors to get them to participate in this neighbor interview:

"I'm helping your neighbor sell their home, and people that are interested in buying want to know what it's like to live in this neighborhood. So, I thought I would ask the neighbors why they love living here."

Help!
Video Tutorials
Chapter 7 provides a step-by-step guide for video editing

This QR link provides a video tutorial on editing using Camtasia

GRAND OPEN HOUSE **PREP**

I let the neighbors share their thoughts with me, and if it sounds good, I'll say, "This is awesome! I'm putting together a social media video about their home and your community and what you said would really help potential buyers with their decision to buy here. Could I use my phone and this tripod to record what you just said? I'll stand next to you and ask the question, 'What do you like about living in this neighborhood?' You can talk to me instead of looking into the camera. We do this all the time."

"I got over a thousand views from my first video and 32 new subscriptions to my website. Then my neighbor's friend I interviewed called me to help her find a home."
- Aceneth Warner, Realtor©

You will want to downplay the video as something simple that's only going on social media. Don't make a big deal out of it or you'll scare them away. The video interview format also makes it easy for them to share without getting nervous. Talking to you is much easier than looking directly at a camera. There's no script, just a simple question, "Why do you like living here?"

If they can do it, you can too
These are examples from agents making their first **Video Home Show** with their smart phone

Sometimes I'll throw in a little of what I'm looking for, like schools, parks, amenities, and access to shopping and restaurants. Afterward, make sure to FRIEND them on Facebook and Instagram so you can tag them on the video.

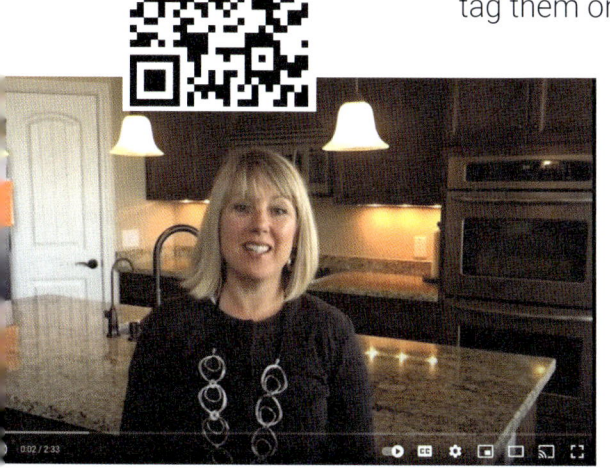

I'll provide more instructions on editing and publishing your videos in Chapter 7 and in the live class, **Become the Community Go-to Agent**. You can also visit our **Help** section and our Facebook Page for recorded instructional videos on how to film and edit.

You can film, edit, and publish this **Video Home**

75

©2023 All rights reserved. Confidential and Proprietary. Intercap Lending, Inc.

GRAND **OPEN HOUSE**

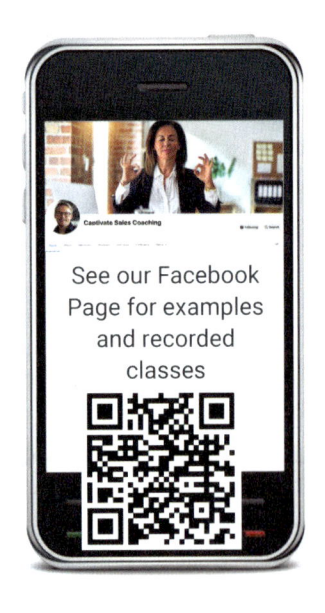

Show in less than an hour once you've done it a few times. When you consistently meet your goal of four new listings a month, you can afford to hire a marketing assistant to edit and publish your videos, boost your ads, post to your Facebook groups, schedule your contractors, get your open house ready, and many other administrative tasks that you should delegate. This is how you grow your business. Refer to the **Listing SOP** at the end of this chapter for a check list of your deliverables.

OPEN HOUSE TIMING

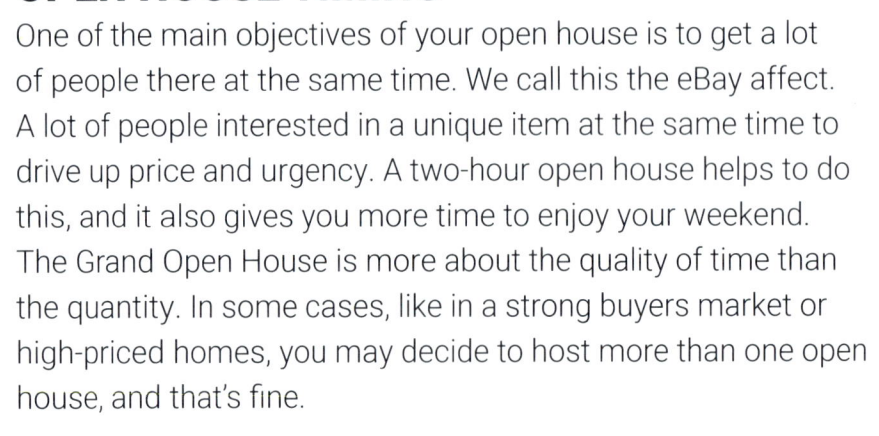

One of the main objectives of your open house is to get a lot of people there at the same time. We call this the eBay affect. A lot of people interested in a unique item at the same time to drive up price and urgency. A two-hour open house helps to do this, and it also gives you more time to enjoy your weekend. The Grand Open House is more about the quality of time than the quantity. In some cases, like in a strong buyers market or high-priced homes, you may decide to host more than one open house, and that's fine.

In most cases, I prefer a Saturday, 11am to 1pm open house. You may also want to consider Sunday mid-mornings or even weekdays 5-7 pm in downtown urban areas. Try a few different times or talk with other agents in your area to get a feel for the best open house times.

Make sure your open house shows on the MLS, Zillow, Trulia, Realtor.com and your social media posts with the correct date and time. I also like to post open house posts on LinkedIn and send an email to all the agents I know. You can even advertise your open house on Eventbrite. This is on top of the five listing advertisements we discussed in the last chapter.

See our Facebook Page for examples and recorded classes

A WELL ADVERTISED 2-HOUR OPEN HOUSE IS ALL YOU NEED

OPEN HOUSE SIGNAGE

This is a grand event, so you should have lots of open house signs, like 20 to 30. Your neighborhood directional signs should help visitors navigate to the home, making sure there is no doubt they've arrived at the right place. Your signs should also advertise you, so make sure they are uniquely branded. Your interior open house signage will guide visitors through the home with two strategic stopping points to help you meet visitors and capture new opportunities.

The most important sign is the front yard **For Sale** sign, which should go up the day you list the home. It's worth the money to invest in a high-quality, full-size post sign with a professionally designed placard. A short metal yard sign does not reflect a **$20,000 Listing Service**.

DIRECTIONAL SIGNS

Your neighborhood open house signs should be easy to spot. You will want three 12-foot tall open house feather flags (see image on right), one for the front of the house, and one at each of the two main entrances of the neighborhood. Do not use balloons! Your Grand Open House is not a kids birthday party.

Place large directional yard signs (see image on left) every 25 yards or so and before every turn in the neighborhood, leading visitors to the house from the tall feather flags. Visitors should never have to guess which direction to go to arrive at your open house.

Place your neighborhood signs a couple

Open House Kit
Order a personally-branded open house kit

GRAND OPEN HOUSE **PREP**

hours before the open house, and take them down within an hour or so after it ends. This will help avoid lost signs, annoyed neighbors, and HOA violations. You shouldn't leave your signs overnight unless you have permission from the city or HOA.

FRONT DOOR SIGN

Even though your directional signs give visitors every indication that this is an open house, many will knock on the door unless you have a sign on the front door that says, "**Open House. Come in.**" The last place you should be is at the door letting people in. You have a more important job to do.

VISITOR STATIONS

Inside the house, you will want to setup two stations to control the flow of visitors and give buyers and agents what they need to make an offer. Your job is to roam between the two stations as you get to know your visitors and answer questions about the home. The first station is the **Shoe Cover Station**. The second is the **Kitchen Show Stopper**.

SHOE COVER STATION

The purpose of this station is to get your visitors to stop in an open area by the front door, like a foyer or front parlor, and put on shoe covers or take off their shoes. Make sure to have a large sign that directs them to do this, with adequate seating for at least 4-5 people.

This station is the best place to introduce yourself as the listing agent. It will give you a moment to get to know your visitors as they sit and put on their shoe covers. You will have three type of visitors at your open house:

1. Represented buyers
2. Unrepresented buyers
3. Neighbors, friends, and looky-loos

78

©2023 All rights reserved. Confidential and Proprietary. Intercap Lending, Inc.

GRAND **OPEN HOUSE**

Represented Buyers

If agents are there with her buyers, speak directly to the agent. You don't want agents to think you are after their clients. Thank them for coming and direct them to the **Kitchen Station**. You can say something like this to the agent, "Please register in the kitchen. You don't need to add your clients. I'll send you links to the 3D tour, floor plans, drone, and a neighbor interview talking about the community that you can share. I also left a clip board with the MLS listing sheet. Please let me know if you have any questions about the home or making an offer. I'll make sure the transaction on my end is fast and smooth. I'd love to work with you."

Unrepresented Buyers

Obviously, you want to get to know this group well. Introduce yourself as the listing agent and say something like this, "In the kitchen is a registration iPad. If you register, I'll send you links to a 3D tour of this home, drone footage, floor plans, and an interview with a neighbor who talks about living in this neighborhood. This will help you remember what you saw and you can share these links with family and friends. As you can imagine, I'm happy to help you make an offer on this home or look at others. I'm an expert in this area. Please come see me after the tour and let's figure out how I can help."

Neighbors, Friends and Looky-loos

Get excited about neighbors and looky-loos. Impress them, keep in touch, and they will be your future clients. If they know the owners, say something like this, "The Johnsons are going to be so happy that you came! I'm going to post some open house pictures on social media to

GRAND **OPEN HOUSE**

share with them. Can I take a picture with you?" After you take the picture, say something like, "Let me send you a FRIEND request so I can tag you. Do you use Facebook or Instagram? Oh, and don't forget to register in the kitchen. I did a neighbor interview with Susan Smith and I'm giving away a dinner for two at Sol Agave."

KITCHEN STATION

Your kitchen station should stop visitors in their tracks, like an Expo display. Make sure your setup reflects your high-value listing service. Here are some ideas:

- Place a digital device (i.e. iPad) on a stand for the open house registrations, with a nicely designed sign that says, "Register to receive a 3D tour, floor plans, drone footage, and an interview with a neighbor talking about the community. Also, a chance to win dinner for two at a great local restaurant called [name]." Total Expert provides digital open house registrations that can automatically send these links and add contacts to your database.

- Provide 5-10 clip boards with an attached pen next to a stack of printed flyers. On one side of the flyer, print the actual MLS listing sheet. This provides all the important details about the home. On the other side, print your standard open house flyer with your picture and information. Total Expert has several Open House flyer templates that can automatically pull pictures and home details from your listing.

- Provide branded water bottles and wrapped treats. Don't skimp on the quality of the treats, and don't provide any open food that could make a mess.

Open House Digital Registration with Total Expert

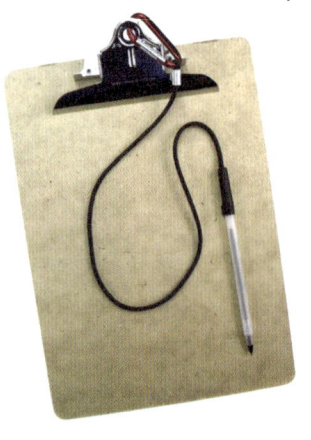

GRAND **OPEN HOUSE**

DURING THE OPEN HOUSE

If you have any VIP registrations from Eventbrite, you are going to let them in 30 minutes before the scheduled open house. Follow the same recommendations of getting to know these VIP visitors while they put on their shoe covers. After they move on to the kitchen, it's time to do a Facebook Live video.

FACEBOOK LIVE

Your Facebook Live video has a lot of value. It shows the seller how great their open house looks since they are not there, it reminds those who saw your Facebook ads that today is the day, and it advertises you as the best listing agent in the area. Here are the steps to doing a Facebook Live video:

- Open your Facebook app on your phone and click the blue video icon for a live video.

- Start by introducing yourself and the open house: "Hi, this is [your name]. I'm at this Grand Open House at [address]." Walk out the front door and show the signs in the front yard. "You can't miss the house. Just follow the signs." Walk up to the front door and show the **Open House. Come In.** sign. "Walk right in and make sure to put on shoe covers. This house is nice!" As you walk towards the kitchen say, "Make sure to register to get links to a 3D tour, floor plans, drone, and an interview with a neighbor. Grab a cookie and check out this amazing [4 bed, 3 bath home in neighborhood]." You can show a little bit of the kitchen and front living room, but don't do a tour. You want them to come see the home in person.

- Save the Facebook video to your phone and post it to Instagram. Make sure to tag the sellers and your partners.

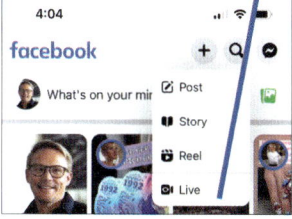

Facebook Live
Open the Facebook app and look for the + button on the top right

Live is the last option in the drop down menu

BE A GOOD HOST
Here are the steps to being a good host that captures more business and shows off your sales skills.

- Be the best dressed person so no one has to guess who is in charge. Wear a name tag so visitors don't forget your name.

- Be present and attentive with visitors. Take pictures with neighbors, people walking through the home (don't show faces), and some pictures of your signs and stations. You are going to share these pictures and video later.

- Follow the earlier recommendations of getting to know your visitors and encouraging them to register and meet with you for help. Be confident that all unrepresented buyers are your future clients.

- Take notes about the people you meet so you can update their registration information or register for them.

AFTER THE OPEN HOUSE
Here are a few suggestions to wrap up your Grand Open House.

- Post all the pictures you took to your Facebook and Instagram business pages. Tag your sellers, partners, and everyone involved. Tag neighbors too.

- Leave the sellers some cookies and a Thank You card. In the card, share how the open house went, like how many people came and what feedback you got about the home. I bring a portable 4x6" printer and print out several of the open house pictures and put them in the card.

- Leave the shoe covers and sign for future showings. This also reminds the sellers of the care you gave their home.

- Take down your open house signs as soon as you are able.

OPEN HOUSE **CHECK LIST**

	2-3 feather flags
	15-20 yard signs
	"Come on in" door sign
	"Please remove or cover your shoes" sign with chairs or bench
	50 - 100 printed MLS sheets with Open House flyer printed on the back
	5 - 10 clipboards with attached pen
	Sign that reads: "Please register to receive 3D tour, drone, and neighbor interview…and a chance to win dinner from…"
	Registration form or digital registration device
	Wrapped cookies or snacks with attached business card
	Water bottles
	Notepad to take names and notes about visitors

Key things to remember

- Be the best dressed person at the open house.
- Wear a name tag so visitors remember your name.
- Take lots of pictures and video.
- Write down names and details of everyone you meet. Try to get their name, phone number, and at least one key detail about every person that comes to your open house.
- Be respectful of other agents and their clients. Speak directly to the agent.
- Spend quality time with the neighbors. Thank them for supporting the seller. Friend them on Facebook. Ask to take pictures. Make an appointment to meet and discuss their real estate needs and aspirations.

LISTING **CHECK LIST**

☐ **1. Listing Report**

☐ **2. Staging**
Houses that look their best sell faster and for more money.

    ☐ **Curb appeal**

    ☐ **Clean and deodorize**

    ☐ **De-clutter and stage**

☐ **3. Video Home Show**
Film and edit your Video Home Show and Neighbor Interview.

☐ **4. Tour, drone, and pictures**
Contact a real estate photography service that also offers drone and Matterport.

☐ **5. MLS, Zillow, and Single Property Website**
Use your best pictures and description. Master the art of the listing.

    ☐ **List on MLS**

    ☐ **Claim Zillow and Realtor.com listings.**
    Make sure these sites are updated with pics, 3d tour, and you as the listing agent.

    ☐ **Create Single Property Website**

☐ **6. Advertise Online**
Create five Facebook posts on your Facebook Business Page and boost them. Carefully word your hook and call to action, pointing to the EventBrite event and Single Property Website.

    ☐ **EventBrite and Facebook Event**

    ☐ **Single Property Website**

    ☐ **Branded 3D tour**

    ☐ **Drone video**

    ☐ **Video Home Show**

LISTING **CHECK LIST**

☐ **7. Advertise in the community**
Door hangers, open house signs, and neighbor interviews are a great way to get the neighbors excited about the open house and learn more about you for their real estate needs.

☐ **8. Signage**
Place signs two hours before the open house

- ☐ **Directional signage**
- ☐ **Yard and door signage**
- ☐ **Interior signage - stations**

☐ **9. Shoe Cover and Kitchen Stations**

- ☐ **Seating and shoe covers**
- ☐ **Hot sheet and flyer print-outs with clip boards**
- ☐ **Wrapped treat with business cards and water bottles**
- ☐ **Registration sheet or tablet with sign**

☐ **10. Facebook Live**
Do a Facebook Live video 15-30 minutes before open house. Post saved video to Instagram

☐ **11. Facebook and Instagram posts - after the open house**
Remove open house links on existing posts and add open house pictures.

☐ **12. Follow-up**

- ☐ **Open house gift to seller - Thank You card, pictures and cookies**
- ☐ **Contact all unrepresented buyers, neighbors, and visitors**
- ☐ **Follow-up email, text, and call to buyer agents**

6

CAPTIVATING BUYERS

CHAPTER SIX
Captivating Buyers

Today's home buyers do their shopping online. To some degree, this has led to agents competing over buyers who are simply trying to get in a door with buyers who aren't that concerned which agent gets the commission or how much they get paid, since the buyer is not paying their agent directly.

Online lead generation of buyers requesting to get into homes has become big business. For many agents, not having to negotiate a buyer commission (commonly thousands of dollars) is a good way to make a living. Some of the most successful real estate teams spend hundreds of thousands of dollars a year on buyer leads, which is a multi-billion-dollar industry. How quickly the agent responds to a buyer lead is the name of the game, with a substantial payout of usually 2-3% of the home's value if the agent can close the deal.

Our research shows that today's buyers work with over three agents in the course of shopping for a new home. If the agent's role is to open a door of a house that the buyer found online, the agent's availability to open that door is king. In a world where we order food from our car and use apps to find the closest ride-share, waiting very long for something we want is not a common virtue. Some buyers we interviewed said they felt guilty calling another agent to see a different home, but admitted that this sense of obligation wasn't as strong if the agent didn't get back to them right away.

Many of these top buyer teams recruit brand new agents who are willing to be the most available agent. The money is great, with little to no experience required to open a door and write a contract. Unfortunately, this approach can get tiring and many agents want to graduate from working every day and hour to keep their clients happy.

The natural evolution of this online buyer lead generation is leads getting more competitive as agents and teams try to grow their piece of the pie, and as real estate lead websites try to grow their market share. There are only so many buyers out there at any given time, and competition for these buyer leads keeps growing. What

CAPTIVATING **BUYERS**

this teaches buyers is that they should find the house they want on these popular websites, and there will be plenty of agents ready and eager to let them in the door and submit an offer. We've interviewed dozens of buyers who think signing a contract with a single buyer agent isn't in their best interest until they get an accepted offer.

The end result: Buyer agents scramble to open doors for a hopeful big payout while our industry suffers the black eye of agents getting paid too much for what they do (at least that's how sellers see it). And then there are agents who do a lot of work they never get paid for, trying to convert leads and keep buyers tied to them until they close. Being competitive on the buyer's side involves round the clock lead management and a lot of persistence.

I can only imagine the look of disappointment on your face as you read this because I've taught this in person to many agents. To be clear, there is nothing wrong with purchasing buyer leads and mastering buyer lead conversion. There's also nothing wrong with not paying for leads at all. The difference with the Captivate approach is taking new buyers, however you capture them, through your homeowner lifecycle so they stick with you from that time forward. This is different from a sales pipeline approach. Captivate helps define some specific best practices to make the buyer experience so good that buyers stick with you while they shop for homes and come back the next time they want to buy or sell. In this chapter, I'm going to show you how to:

- Capture buyers before they start looking for a home.
- Use **Insider Information** and **Distinctive Homes** to keep buyers shop with you, and no one else, until they go under contract.
- Use technology that keeps buyers tied to you as they drive neighborhoods and continue looking at homes online.
- Celebrate the purchase with a **Signing** and **Dinner Party**.
- Provide buyers with home maintenance reminders and home service provider recommendations after they buy.
- Give buyers a monthly home digest showing the home's estimated value and the owner's home equity.

CAPTIVATING BUYERS

Let's run through this Captivate buyer offering like a typical buyer lead workflow. For this exercise, we'll start with buyers coming in from a showing request, meaning they found a home online and they contacted you to look at it. Once we run the buyer through their first purchase, we'll review how to keep them coming back.

STEP 1: You get a new buyer lead, "I want to see a house I found online."

On my wall is a reminder of my Captivate mission statement, "Create Raving Fans." This reminds me that my goal is to give everyone I meet a reason to work with me from that point forward. So, without any qualifying questions, I say, "Great! I'll make an appointment. When would you like to see it?"

Now that they know I'm available to make an appointment and show the home, I ask a few questions to better understand their story. Primarily what they want in a new home and when they want to move. I'll also get them registered for text and email listing alerts. You know the drill.

Once I get their name, contact information, and desired showing time, I say something like, "This is a three bed, 2 bath townhome in Vineyard for $420,000. I'm looking at the pictures now. This is a great place. What do you like best about this place? Are you looking strictly for townhomes in Vineyard?"

If you've been an agent for any length of time, you don't need me to tell you how to gather their needs and wants list. The goal is to get them to share as much information as possible so you can help them find the right place if this isn't the one. The main things you want to understand are price range, general location, size and type of home, reason for moving, when they want to move, and anything on their wish list.

STEP 2: Next, I print out the MLS listing sheet for the property they want to see, read it thoroughly, and mark anything that stands out with a highlighter. I look for information like HOA fees and benefits, taxes, age of major items (roof, HVAC, etc), agent remarks, and anything that's important or interesting about the property. Buyers miss most of this information when they shop online. On a notepad, I write down questions about any missing information. I do this before I call the agent. This is the start of my **Insider Information**.

STEP 3: I call the listing agent to make the appointment, and I try to get additional information that's not on the listing. I usually start the conversation with something like, "My clients are really excited about your listing," with some details about what they like about the home. Then I ask any questions I noted when I read the MLS sheet. As long as I am positive and courteous, most listing agents are pretty helpful with additional information that's not on the MLS. Getting the listing agent on your side is especially helpful if there are multiple offers or tough negotiations. Listing agents want to work with buyer agents who are polite, good communicators, and mindful of making the deal work for everyone. Before I end the call, I ask the most important question of all, "Is there anything you can tell me that will help my clients make a good offer?"

On the top back of the MLS sheet I write, **Insider Information** in big letters. This is where I add all the additional information I learned from the listing agent. You may be surprised how much insider information you can capture by taking the time to fully review the MLS sheet and having a good conversation with the listing agent. You will get to know other agents in your area well, so always be polite and professional because your paths will likely cross again.

STEP 4: I check the MLS for any other properties that are similar to the one the buyers requested. If you find any worth showing, follow the same steps to capture Insider Information. Let your clients know that you confirmed the showing for their requested home and you have a couple more similar properties to show them. Also, explain that you have some important insider information about these properties. If they ask, tell them it's information based on research you did on the home. You are teaching your new clients that you have more to offer than simply opening doors and writing offers.

STEP 5: Considering what the buyer shared about their ideal property, I try to pick one or two more properties that gives the buyer more on their wish list, but is likely priced higher or is located outside their preferred area. I call these **Distinctive Homes**. Most buyers get stuck on price and location, and so do their agents. Unfortunately, the buyer's wish list doesn't always match up with their price and location requirements. Here's some interesting insights we found as we implemented Distinctive Homes:

- About 25% of buyers ended up finding a way to afford the property that offered more on their wish list, even though the home was priced above their stated budget or located outside their preferred area. I had an agent send a $1.3M listing to a

CAPTIVATING BUYERS

client who said he couldn't pay over $750,000. She was frustrated that they had spent three months looking at homes around $750,000 and the buyer was never satisfied. The buyer texted back minutes after the agent sent the more expensive listing saying, "This is exactly what I'm looking for." They went under contract that night for $1.2 million.

- The majority of the buyers that saw these distinctive homes decided that they didn't want to pay more for their wish list or live outside their preferred area, but many of them now felt better about what was available. Their indecisiveness and doubt went away with these distinctive homes, and they were able to make a happier and quicker decision to stick with what they could afford in their desired area.

- The rest of the buyers we surveyed were only interested in specific homes. Some felt the agent was helpful in giving them more options while others just wanted to look at the homes they found.

STEP 6: Here is what I do when I arrive at the first showing:

- I have my branded Home Shopping Bag ready with my folder, MLS printouts, and the Loan Consideration Sheets. I also like to include the **Listing Sheets** to show them what I do to sell properties.

- Before I hand them the shopping bag, I take out the MLS sheet for the first property and point out all the insider information I found on the home. I show them the highlighted and written information before the tour. I put this on a clip board so they can look at it and take additional notes as they tour the home.

- I walk through the property with them and take pictures and notes of anything that stands out or they mention. Later, I send them a summary email about each property, including the pictures and notes that I took.

- When I'm done with the first house, I show them the folder with the other MLS sheets. I place them in the order of the showings and show them that each sheet

CAPTIVATING **BUYERS**

CAPTIVATE Tote

Captivate Store
Order a custom-branded Home Shopping Bag and Folders

Help! Video Tutorials
Learn how to create **Listing Sheets** with Total Expert

has **Insider Information** highlighted and written on the back. I put the folder in the shopping bag and hand it to them so they can preview these properties before we arrive. I also put water bottles and snacks in the shopping bag.

- At the end of the showings, I usually have a good idea if they are ready to submit an offer. If not, I let them know that I took pictures and notes on each home, and I'll send them a summary. I remind them that they will get text and email alerts from me with new listings and I'll try to have new homes to look at each week. I also give them the Homebuyer App and show them how to view all the homes for sale in the area as they drive around neighborhoods.

Before we part ways, I have them sign the buyer's agreement. I rarely get any objections. If I do, I explain that I don't get paid until they purchase and this agreement is my commitment to helping them find the right home. I also encourage them to get fully approved for a loan, and if not, invite them to meet with my lender partner to get a pre-approval letter and explain what that means.

This might seem like a lot of work, and it is! This is what separates you from other buyer agents in terms of your quality of buyer services. These efforts should help you retain and capture more buyers, so the extra work is worth it. The Distinctive Homes and Insider Information also help buyers make faster and better decisions.

Your technology will help keep buyers tied to you in between showings. These include the traceable listing alerts from your agent website and the Homebuyer App, which I will cover next.

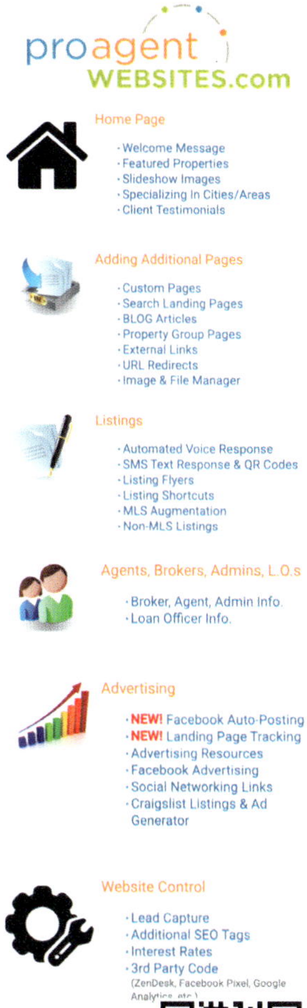

CAPTIVATING BUYERS

AGENT WEBSITE AND LISTING ALERTS (HOT SHEETS)

As I mentioned in the Digital Marketing chapter, an IDX agent website provides all the listings in your MLS on your personal website. A good agent website also helps you manage your buyers with text and email listing alerts, home search tracking, and showing requests. If you don't have your own website that provides these features, I recommend **Pro Agent Websites**. You can't beat the cost for what you get (use the QR code on the left for a discount).

The Pro Agent's Buyer Lead Dashboard is where you manage your buyers. You can send listing alerts via text and email and see which buyers are active on your site.

Captivate has partnered with **Pro Agent Websites** to provide a discounted website hosting service ($20/month savings) with added support. There are lots of video tutorials to help you use this agent website to stay in touch with your buyers as they shop online. You can even send personal video emails.

Visit www.proagentwebsites.com/Intercap for more information.

HOMEBUYER APP

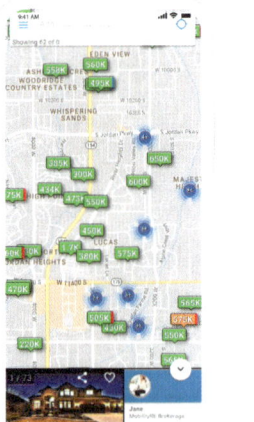

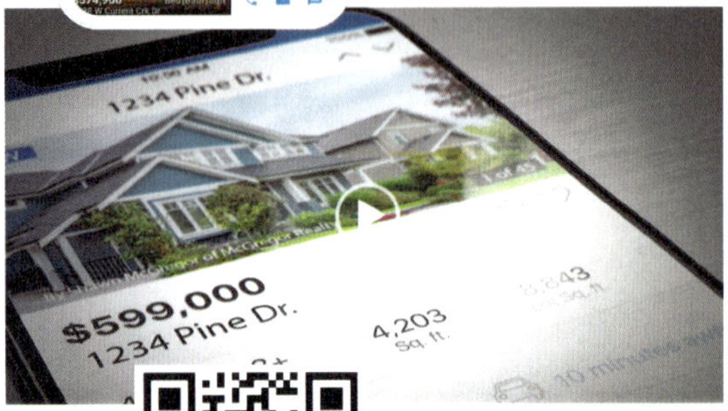

PREAPPROVAL	HOME SHOPPING	UNDER CONTRACT	CLOSING
Use the mortgage calculator, apply and get pre-approved for a home loan	Browse homes and let your agent know which ones you want to look at	Upload and sign documents and receive loan status updates	Review the closing disclosures and get ready to sign

Homebuyer App
View more details and request a free license

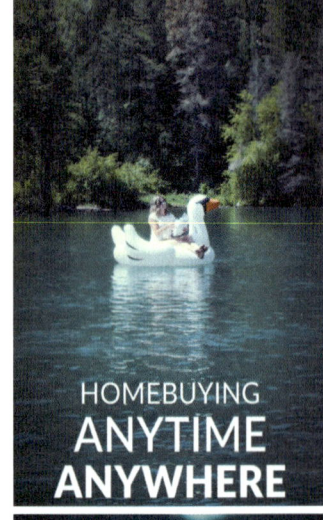

The **Home Buyer App** is the portable version of online home shopping. It's a phone app that allows buyers to view listings on their phone, with the added advantage of using the phone's GPS so buyers can view property pictures, videos, and information of the homes that are around them. It's an MLS listing site with you as their buyer agent. Buyers can favorite properties, request showings, or ask a question, all going to you. Buyers can also use a built-in mortgage calculator, compare loan options, and even apply for a loan with the app.

Home buyers like to drive around the neighborhoods where they want to live. For Sale signs typically don't provide information about the home, so buyers go to popular online real estate websites on their phone to get more information. These sites encourage buyers to contact their agents for a showing. The listing signs also entice the buyer to contact the listing agent. The Homebuyer App is a must-have to keep your buyers tied to you while they drive neighborhoods. Use the QR code link to the left to get setup with the Homebuyer App.

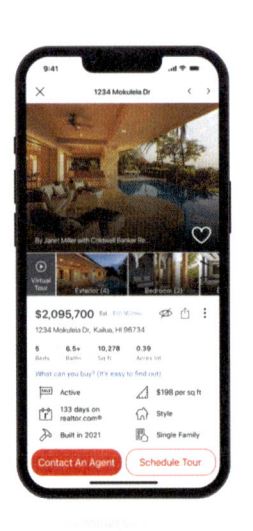

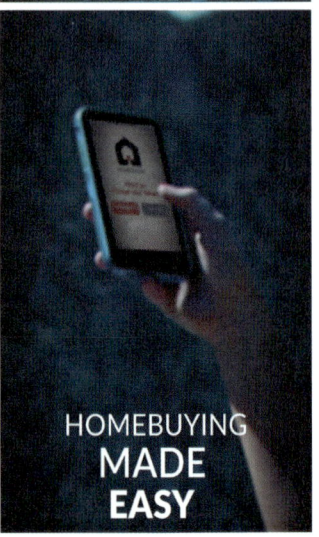

HOMEBUYING ANYTIME ANYWHERE

HOMEBUYING MADE EASY

©2023 All rights reserved. Confidential and Proprietary. Intercap Lending, Inc.

CAPTIVATING **BUYERS**

Writing Offers

Negotiating the best offer for your client can be tricky. Open communication with the listing agent can help you understand what the seller might accept. It's usually not a good idea to throw out an offer and hope it sticks. First, learn what your clients want to offer and then start a dialogue with the listing agent, if he or she is willing. Any insight to possible concessions and pricing considerations from the listing agent will go a long way towards negotiating a deal that both parties can accept. Nothing is agreed upon until both parties sign, so don't count on anything until it's legally binding.

> YOUR VALUES AND ETHICS ARE PART OF YOUR BRAND IDENTITY

Your client may be emotional about the purchase. Your job is to be factual and level-headed. Ultimately, follow your client's wishes and never compromise your fiduciary duties. Don't let the emotion of a closed deal and commission check negatively impact your decision to do what is right. Your ethics and values are in integral part of your brand identity, and will keep you out of trouble.

There's a lot more to consider than this quick review of negotiating the best deal. Tim Burrell, a real estate agent, coach, and lawyer published a book called, "**Create A Great Deal, The Art of Real Estate Negotiating**." I highly recommend it.

Once you get an accepted offer, you've got a short time to celebrate before you get busy with the **Under Contract** stage of the lifecycle. The job's not done until you close. I'm not going to review the standard real estate tasks and paperwork here. Work with your broker or team lead if you need help with this process. However, I want to touch on the communication between you, your client, the lender, and Title during this under contract stage.

Going under contract doesn't mean you pass the baton to the lender and escrow officer and hope for the best. This is

CAPTIVATING **BUYERS**

a time for your to show that you are still leading this team in the best interest of your shared client. There's a reason that this coaching program is a dual effort between a committed mortgage company and their real estate partners. Intercap Lending views their real estate partners as the sales lead and primary client representative. Your Intercap loan officers count on you as much as you count on them while your client is under contract.

The **Homebuyer App** will keep you and the client apprised of loan status updates, document requests, and other loan requirements. The app even allows borrowers to take pictures of their documents and upload them securely to their loan file. E-sign is also integrated into the loan workflow.

Hopefully, your client was approved for a mortgage by their Intercap loan officer before you submitted an offer. This will help avoid delays and surprises. Intercap offers a **$1,000 Loan Approval Guarantee** that you can include with the offer letter. I highly recommend that you and your client take advantage of this added value. See more information about this guarantee to the left.

$1,000 Loan Approval Guarantee
Make your offers stronger with an approval guarantee

Loan Status Updates
There are five primary loan status updates that Intercap's systems will automatically send the buyer's agent and the borrower via text and email. These include:
1. Application Accepted
2. Under Contract
3. Underwriting Review
4. Clear-to-close
5. Funded

The first status, Application Accepted, includes a small

CAPTIVATING **BUYERS**

congratulatory gift of a planted tree with the message, "We planted a tree to improve our home as you get ready for your new home." Every step and detail are directed towards high-value services.

There are also several loan updates and assurances that should be conveyed with a personal phone call. Intercap loan officers that participate in the Captivate program are committed to making a weekly loan status update phone call to the borrower and both agents. These lender partners will ensure each party is personally updated with the loan status each week so no one has to guess or worry what's going on. The **Under Contract** stage is one of the most stressful periods of homeownership. Pro-active communication by the lender is key to a quick and smooth closing without the stress. Intercap Lending has become so good at this process, they beat the industry close-time average by two weeks and maintain a 4.97 out of 5 star review rating from Zillow and Google with over 16,000 reviews[1].

SIGNING PARTY

It's finally time to sign, but why are settlements such a boring conclusion to a home purchase? In the book, **Power of Moments**, Chip Heath suggests that, "Moments are what we remember and what we cherish. Certainly we might celebrate achieving a goal, such as completing a marathon or landing a significant client—but the achievement is embedded in a moment. And defining moments are the ones that endure in our memories.[2]"

Let's change boring settlements into memorable celebrations of a new home purchase. Here is what Captivate agents do:

CELEBRATE THE SIGNING WITH YOUR CLIENTS

Signing Party
Turn your settlement into a signing party

---

1 Based on loans funded January 1, 2022 through December 31st, 2022. Review rating as of January 2023.
2 The Power of Moments: Why Certain Experiences Have Extraordinary Impact, by Chip Heath

CAPTIVATING **BUYERS**

- Throw a little party at the signing table. Bring a cake, champagne glasses, fancy finger foods, whatever you want to make the settlement a celebration. This has been so successful, the Title company I use created party packages that agents can choose for their **Signing Party.**

- Give your clients a hand-written thank you card that invites them to a **Dinner Party** with a note that you will give their house warming gift at the party (I'll explain that next). Have them open the card and commit to the dinner date. Make a big deal out of it. It's best to have them put the dinner party on their calendar now so they don't forget.

- Explain that a lot of your business comes from reviews and referrals, and if that was the case here, remind them of that. Ask if they wouldn't mind taking a minute before they leave to give you a review. Text them your Zillow and Google review links. Make sure you have these links ready. You will get more and better reviews if they do it at the settlement table with you there.

THE DINNER PARTY IS YOUR INTIMATE CLIENT APPRECIATION EVENT

CLOSING DINNER PARTY

DINNER PARTY

Think of the signing party as the wedding and the dinner party as the reception. Two defining moments to a home sale or purchase that your clients will remember until they need your help again. Here's how to host a **Captivate Dinner Party**.

CAPTIVATING **BUYERS**

Client Dinner Party
Invite clients and those who referred them

- Pick a favorite restaurant that you reserve every month — same date and time, like the third Thursday at 6:30 pm. This way you don't have to plan something different every month. It's one of your time blocks we'll cover in the eighth chapter.

- Meet with the restaurant owner or manager and explain that you plan to have a client dinner there every month at the same day/time that will consist of all the clients who bought or sold a home with you that month. Notify the restaurant a few days ahead of time with the expected number of guests. Explain that you are also introducing new homeowners to their restaurant and try to negotiate a discount.

- See if you can reserve a private room or relatively private area of the restaurant. Keep in mind that the owner, manager, waiters and others may be your future clients. You are going to get to know them all very well as they see you in action. Be gracious and tip generously. You might be surprised how well this pays off over time.

- Each month you are going to invite your clients who closed since the last Dinner Party, and anyone who referred them. I recommend a client couple, or if single with a plus-one (not the whole family). Also invite anyone who referred that client and their plus-one. If you don't close a deal in a month, bring your significant other or friend and make a new commitment to follow Captivate, because diligent Captivate agents never have a goose-egg month!

- Have appetizers on the table and see if a waiter can take drink orders as guests arrive. You want your guests to mingle, not sit and look at a menu. Introduce your guests, and if it won't offend them, what they accomplished. "John and Susie just bought their dream home and John got his gourmet kitchen. Kevin just graduated and bought his first

CAPTIVATING BUYERS

place." Be careful not to share anything personal, but try to keep the spirit of a celebration. Hopefully, your guests are all pleasantly surprised at how much business you do.

- To control costs, you can work with the restaurant to create your own special menu with limited choices and without listed prices. This way you can manage your budget better. You can also ask your lender, title rep, home warranty, and other strategic partners to join you and pay a portion of the cost. The cost of the meal is part of your closing gift to the client, so budget accordingly.

- During desert, hand out the house warming gifts. Get some specialty spices for the cook that got their dream kitchen or a dish set for the first-time buyer. We found that wrapping the gifts make the moment even more special. Give a gift to those who referred your clients too. Best to make it a compliant SWAG gift, but something they would love to have. You can put your logo on just about anything, like a wine bottle. After the gifts, it's time to thank everyone and set your team up for the next time. Here's a suggestion:

"Next to you on the table is a packet with some information about some recommended local contractors, from lawn care to home remodeling and maid services. There's even a discount for this restaurant. Our businesses," (considering you have partners with you), "are built on good people like you. Thank you! We hope you had a good time tonight and we would love to see you here again. There's this interesting phenomenon that when we do something significant, like buy a home, we hear about others trying to do the same thing. It's like when you buy a car and start seeing that same make and model everywhere. We're hoping that when you hear from others who need help with real estate, you'll recommend us. And then like [referrer name at dinner], we'll invite you to the next dinner. We've also

Dinner Party Menu

Create your own dinner menu to control costs and promote your brand

CAPTIVATING **BUYERS**

included our information on a fridge magnet. That way you don't forget how to get a hold of us. We are also going to send you a monthly home equity statement so you can track your home investment. We are here for you, anytime. We hope to see you soon."

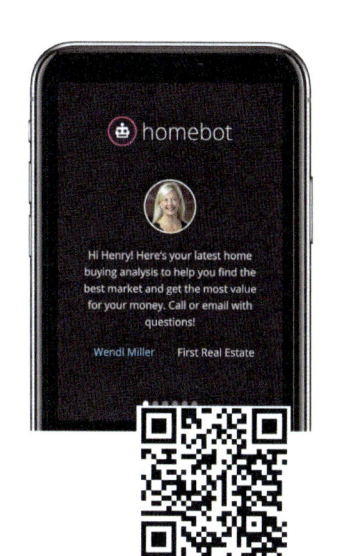

POST-CLOSE SUPPORT
Throughout the years between home purchases, Captivate agents and their partners have ongoing discussions with their clients about equity, home improvements, personal finances, second homes, next homes, and property investments. Your Homebot Digest will give clients a monthly snapshot of their home's value and equity to help them consider these options. If your routines and technologies are in place, you should know when your clients and SOI want to make a move, and the support you continue to offer will position you as their first point of contact for all things related to real estate.

Top-of-mind, forget-me-not marketing is no longer needed to capture new business from your SOI. Your monthly Home Equity Statement (Homebot), social media listing advertisements, Facebook group posts, and other occasional posts about the housing market, new loan program options, and home maintenance reminders will be more than enough to remind a growing group of followers of your high-value services.

In the next chapter, I will also introduce you to community farming using video and social media, and in Chapter 8, I'll introduce you to the **Captivate Power Hour** to help you build a routine for keeping in touch with your SOI on a regular basis as they navigate through the homeowner lifecycle.

Home Value & Equity Digest
Send your clients a monthly digest of their home's value and equity

7

COMMUNITY GO-TO AGENT

CHAPTER SEVEN
Community Go-to Agent

When I ask agents what they believe their clients value most when choosing a real estate agent, the typical answers are trust, communication, experience, availability, and real estate knowledge. We've already established that availability is important to buyers. However, what we found in our research is that these qualities are expectations to our clients, not what sets an agent apart. We surveyed over 20,000 homeowners and found that **community expertise** is what buyers and sellers considered most important when choosing an agent. Our clients expect us to be trustworthy, good communicators, know what we are doing, and readily available to help. What they believe will give them an added advantage is community expertise.

In the same survey, we asked homeowners what they considered when buying a home. We took their answers and came up with a top-five list in order of importance:

1. Community or location where they want to live
2. Commute to work
3. Schools the kids will attend
4. The home (size, layout, age, condition)
5. Community amenities (shopping, parks, golf course, lake, restaurants, etc)

The most revealing part of these results is that the home came in fourth place, and things like the home's size, layout, age, and condition were all lumped together under one consideration. Once buyers decide where they want to live and what community amenities they value, the available homes in that area within their budget are good enough. Do you know clients who settled on a home based more on the communities they loved or the schools the kids would go to, than the home itself? Buyers still want a nice home, and one that checks as many wish list boxes as possible, but they accept what they can afford in the communities they prefer.

We have millennials buying small studio condominiums for hundreds of dollars per square foot just to be in the heart of downtown, close to work and their favorite coffee shops, clubs, schools, friends, and shopping centers. Understanding the communities where you serve is as important as understanding the overall housing market in the greater area.

When email blasts and online marketing made their way into real estate over two decades ago, many agents stopped being true community experts. Agents broadened their footprint to multiple cities and sometimes across state lines. I know agents who drive a hundred miles or more a day as they traverse across large areas to help their clients. These agents have a general knowledge of the communities they serve, but nothing in depth. I'm talking about names of school administrators and specific school programs, local mom-and-pop stores and restaurants, and local biking and hiking trails.

> FARMING IS ABOUT GOING DEEP INSTEAD OF BROAD AS A REAL ESTATE MARKETING STRATEGY

Before you shudder at the thought of limiting your work area to a small city, what I'm suggesting is developing a new marketing strategy for geographic farming. You can continue to work in as large of an area as you need to keep the deals coming in, but I will help you give new clients a reason to choose you over other agents, not because you do what every other agent does, but because you have community expertise that makes you stand out from most agents.

If you do this right, you may find that a bigger percentage of your clients and SOI become concentrated in a smaller geographic area. Going deep instead of broad in your marketing campaigns can have a bigger impact on your business than you may realize. Let other agents work large markets while you dominate a small city or community. The other side benefits of this hyper-local approach include fewer miles on your car, less money in gas, and a shorter workday.

To get started with this community marketing strategy, let's define a geographic farm and a niche farm. You should have one of each.

BECOME THE GO-TO AGENT IN YOUR GEOGRAPHIC AND NICHE FARM

Geographic Farm

A geographic farm is a specific area where you market your real estate expertise, usually a town or small to mid-size city. The goal is to be a real estate expert in the following:

1. Neighborhoods (subdivisions, developments, master plan communities, 55+ communities, high-density complexes, acreage properties, horse properties, airbnb and ADU-friendly communities, etc)
2. Schools (public and private schools, universities, specialty programs, sports teams, charters, day care, vocational training, college prep, clubs, extra curricular programs, etc)
3. Commute to work (public transportation, traffic conditions, alternative routes, ride shares, and proximity to highways)
4. All homes for sale and rent in your farm
5. Community amenities (sport leagues, parks, golf courses, lakes, shopping, restaurants, trails, entertainment, etc)

If your farm is too large or too small, these considerations have less meaning, so pick a farm where the people in that area feel like this is their home town. In the case of a geographic farm, I recommend choosing the area where you live since you are likely more invested in that community.

Niche Farm

A niche farm is a particular buyer type, like first-time buyers, luxury home buyers, investors, vacation home buyers, mover-uppers, and down-sizers. Although you can easily help any of these buyer types, understanding why they purchase and what they specifically need is where you can stand above other agents who are not specialists. Investors need local contractors, insurance agents, accountants, and hard money lenders. They want help calculating CAP rates and average rental income. First-time buyers need affordable living and knowledge of what it takes to qualify for a mortgage. First-time buyer programs and house hacking options are helpful to first-time buyers. Each buyer type has specific needs and

> HYPER-LOCAL MARKETING GIVES BUYERS AND SELLERS A REASON TO CHOOSE YOU OVER AGENTS WHO ARE NOT COMMUNITY EXPERTS

COMMUNITY **GO-TO AGENT**

considerations that you can master as a specialist. When choosing a niche farm, I recommend some crossover with your geographic farm. For example, if your geographic farm has a lot of luxury homes, you may want to focus on luxury home buyers. You can also broaden your niche farm's geographic area. For example, you may choose a city for your geographic farm, which includes all buyer types, and the county for the niche farm, which includes a specific buyer type.

Some agents ask me, "Why not work multiple farms?" My answer is you don't have the time and you shouldn't spend the money to market too broadly. This actually defeats the purpose of being a true community and niche expert. Again, you can work with as many buyer types in as many areas as you want, and you likely will, but your marketing campaigns should be hyper-local.

Your farm marketing strategy will have two focuses: **Digital** and **In-person**. Your digital marketing focus will include social media, your website, and online reviews. This is your online presence and it works best when it's hyper-local. We covered some of this digital marketing in Chapter 4, particularly with the Facebook group, **Homes and Rentals in [your farm]**.

Your in-person focus will include getting to know community leaders and the local amenities really well. Community leaders include people like school administrators, civic leaders, local contractors, and local business owners. Local amenities include things like public transportation, event venues, parks, restaurants, golf courses, coffee shops, and other popular places in the area. A lot of what you share online will come from your community relationships and the local amenities.

Hyper-local advertising is usually more affordable than most agents realize. You can do a billboard, mailers, PPC and social

Example of a Pro Agent Website

Pro Agent Website Offer
www.proagentwebsites.com/Intercap

media ads in a concentrated market for a lot less money than you think. Here are your to-do items and needs list to get your farm marketing strategy going:

1. **Agent Website.** Having your own agent website with blogs and search landing pages will help build your hyper-local online content. If you don't have your own site, I recommend Pro Agent Websites (see QR link on the left).
2. **Social Media**. Your social media accounts will help you promote your community expertise (see chapter 4). Facebook, Instagram, and YouTube are the top three social media platforms for real estate marketing.
3. **Smart phone with tripod, microphone and optional stabilizer**. These will help you film community videos and interviews (see chapter 5, Video Home Shows).
4. **Video editor, like Camtasia**. This will allow you to create video content (more information later in this chapter).
5. **Zillow and Google Business Profiles**. These are the best places to get customer reviews and improve local searches as a community real estate agent.

AGENT WEBSITE

In chapters 4 and 5 we talked about some of the advantages of an agent website, like the buyer lead management functions and the MLS listing pages that you can post on your community Facebook group - **Homes for Sale and Rent in [your farm]**. In addition to these features, Pro Agent also offers three types of landing pages: 1. **Search Landing Pages**, 2. **Custom Landing Pages**, and 3. **Blogs**. Each of these will help you create hyper-local content so you can attract leads from online home shoppers looking in your farm area. In addition, A Pro Agent Website allows you to set your **Featured Communities** and **Search Engine Optimization (SEO)** tags so that search engines index your site for these hyper-local searches. None of this hyper-focused content on your website will change the user experience of serving your entire MLS.

Search Landing Pages

COMMUNITY **GO-TO AGENT**

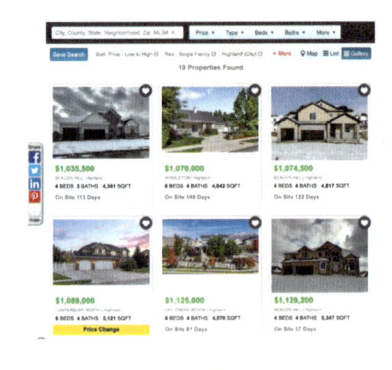

A Search Landing Page is like creating listing alerts for your website that visitors can find when they search online. Most home shoppers don't search for "homes for sale in Colorado." They search, "townhomes for sale in Cherry Creek." These long-tail, hyper-local searches are very common, and the bigger real estate sites cannot optimize for hyper-local real estate content like you can. So, instead of trying to compete with them on general home searches (which you will never get), you can beat them with hyper-local searches if you create a lot of good hyper-local real estate content about your community.

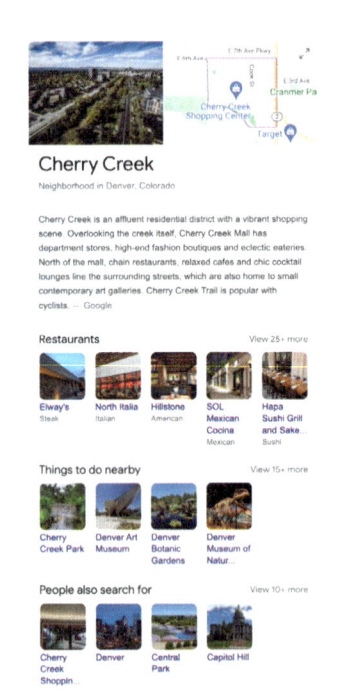

In the admin section of your Pro Agent Website, you can create a landing page that searches the MLS dynamically for very specific types of homes, prices, locations, and even things like horse property and FHA-approved properties. For example, you can create a search landing page that includes all townhomes for sale in Cherry Creek, Colorado. Imagine all of the possible search landing pages you could create for your farm based on property type, price range, house size, lot size, city, neighborhood, and dozens of other specific search criteria. You can even create these MLS search landing pages based on school boundaries. A search landing page only takes a few minutes to create on a Pro Agent Website, and it will dynamically display listings based on the MLS search criteria that you specify, meaning you only have to create the page once and it will continually update with new listings.

Hyper-local Advertising
Home buyers search for specific areas and communities

If you make a goal to create one landing page a day for 6 months, taking just a few minutes a day, you would have 180 hyper-local search landing pages for your farm. The search engines like Google and Bing will index these pages so people searching for those specific types of properties in your farm would find your website at the top of the search request. It takes some time to show up at the top of an organic web search, but it happens because your competition is not optimizing for hyper-local real estate searches like this. Every time you create a new search landing page, you can post that page link on your Facebook Group, **Homes for Sale and Rent in [your farm]**. These search landing pages won't take the place of the individual listings you post each day, but will make a nice addition for neighborhood searches, and create another back link to your website. You can dominate your farm's online presence by building these hyper-local search landing pages.

These hyper-local pages can also be advertised for long-tail key word searches using Pay-per-click (PPC) advertising. This is a great way to generate your own buyer leads in your farm.

Community Influencer Interview
Local high school principal

Custom Landing Pages

Custom landing pages are like search landing pages, but without the MLS listings. These pages are perfect for sharing community amenities in your farm. You can create a custom landing page for each of the schools in your farm, parks, golf courses, hiking trails, restaurants, you name it. There are likely numerous possibilities of local amenities that are worth mentioning within a specific farm area, and each one can have its own custom landing page. You should add pictures, video, and written content on your custom landing page. Custom landing pages can be shared on your Facebook Group and Business Page to showcase the community and your community expertise. These posts get buyers more excited to move to your farm area, and entices sellers who want a community expert to sell their home. These community landing pages and social media posts are also a great way to stay top-of-mind without redundant self-promotion.

Your community content should be original (meaning don't plagiarize or steal pictures), and it's best to involve the people in the community who own or manage these local businesses and services. Imagine yourself as a journalist doing a write-up on the local high school soccer team. You could take pictures,

COMMUNITY **GO-TO AGENT**

Community Amenities
Local restaurant reviews

interview coaches, and dig up insights that only the locals know about. You can visit local restaurants and do a monthly foodie review of all the best places to eat in the area. You can take a Go-pro on biking or hiking trails. There are so many possibilities.

Do one of these community reviews a month and over time you will have every local school program, restaurant, park, and best places to visit on your website. The benefit to your business is worth this hyper-local marketing effort in the following ways:

1. This information is valuable to people who live in the community, want to live there, and the businesses who serve the community. As long as you make your videos and post about the community, you will have an engaged and growing audience. You will get credit as the real estate community expert without having to self-promote.

2. The community leaders that you meet and interview are also home buyers and excellent referral partners. Help them share their community services and they will help you. It's not just a sales or personal advertising approach, this is about helping your clients, future clients, community leaders, partners, and business owners share their love for their community.

3. When you tag and share videos, pictures, and articles about the community, your social media following will grow much faster. This will become your audience for your listing advertisements and Facebook group posts. Pretty soon, you will be a community influencer yourself, and everyone in the community will think of you as the community real estate expert. Talk about referral business!

> BE STRATEGIC ABOUT WHAT YOU DO AND HOW MUCH TIME YOU SPEND DOING IT

Blog Pages
Blogs are the perfect format for covering local news and events, like high school championship games, annual parades, local concerts, and new housing developments. Pick the biggest events of the year in your farm and write a blog about it. You can write something before the event and let people in the community know it's coming, or after the event and post pictures and interviews with those who attended.

How to make this farm strategy work for business growth
This is a name-recognition effort, both for you and the community, which means that you don't get paid for this work and you likely won't benefit from it unless you do it consistently and strategically. When the time comes, these are great tasks for a full-time marketing coordinator between client-focused responsibilities. Until you can hire someone, I recommend making a goal to do one search landing page a week (10 min), one custom landing page a month (2-3 hours) and a blog when there's a big local event (1-2 hours). If you are going to get help, make sure you are still the director, actor, and author. You have to connect your brand with the community. YOU are the brand.

Another piece of advice: Don't get so excited about building your community brand that you forget to prospect new business as a daily sales effort. This kind of farm marketing is a slow and steady strategy that compliments your daily lead generation and sales strategies. We'll discuss your daily, weekly, and monthly routines for growth in the next chapter.

As you venture out to get to know the community and its influencers, I recommend attending and joining the following local groups or organizations. This is where you will get your best ideas and meet the community leaders:

1. Your Realtor® Association meetings and committees
2. Local Chamber of Commerce
3. City Council Meetings

4. Economic Development Committee in the city council
5. BNI or other business networking groups
6. PTA (if you have children)

If you live and work in the same community, this involvement will feel less like a job or extra work. The thing about real estate is that it has everything to do with the schools, restaurants, parks, city services, and living in a community. As a community expert, you can become an influencer that helps the community grow as your business grows.

> POTENTIAL CLIENTS WANT TO SEE YOU SHARE PICTURES AND VIDEOS OF BEAUTIFUL HOMES AND LOCAL COMMUNITIES

PICTURES AND VIDEO

Your online articles and posts will get a lot more engagement if you use pictures and video regularly. Today's camera phones are remarkably good at taking high-quality pictures and video. When you are out in your community, get used to taking pictures and video of the people and places that make your community great. Share, tag, and check-in on Facebook and Instagram regularly. Be a part of the pictures and video, but don't make them about you. If too many pictures are selfies, and lots of your comments are about you and your business, people will stop paying attention. Make your pictures, videos, posts and comments about the places and people in the community and you will get a lot more attention than if you make them about yourself.

Here are a few things you need to know about publishing good

videos:
- You can do it yourself. You don't need expensive equipment or a professional videographer. As long as you are genuine and helpful (not self-promoting), others will appreciate your videos even if they are not perfect.
- Video publishing is not hard to master, so give yourself a break and don't worry that your first several videos aren't as good as you hoped. You will continue to get better!
- You need to use video in your marketing and sales efforts more often, so don't put it off any longer.
- The biggest hurdle is getting comfortable filming, editing and publishing video regularly. Make it a goal and habit.
- Make sure your sound and lighting are good and video movements are smooth.

Here's a quick tutorial on light, sound, and video editing. You can also find instructional videos with the links to the left.

YOUR POSTS WILL GET MORE ENGAGEMENT IF YOU USE VIDEO

Help!
Video Tutorials
Watch a video on how to make a video

Video Lighting

This used to be an issue, but not anymore. Today's smart phones are amazingly good at adjusting to most any lighting. What you see on your phone is how the video will look.. If you film client videos from your office, like videos that introduce yourself, happy birthday videos, or informational videos, you may want to buy a smart phone light attachment to brighten and evenly tone your face. You can pick these up almost anywhere you find smart phone accessories.

Stabilizing Video

You should have a good tripod and a phone stabilizer so your videos aren't shaky. Look for a tripod that has a smart phone holder. You may want to get a short one for your desktop and a tall one for when you are standing. You want the camera to be at eye level.

When you are moving or filming B-roll (background video), a stabilizer like a DJI Osmo® will keep the video smooth. Bouncy videos are not fun to watch, so make sure to use smooth movements. A stabilizer smooths movements and is well worth the investment.

B-roll Video

B-roll is a supplementary video, secondary to your primary footage. When you are filming a **Video Home Show** or showcasing a local business or event, B-roll is the best way to show your viewers what you are talking about without having to talk and walk at the same time. Think of it like a news broadcaster that sits or stands in one place while providing the news, with video that shows what they are talking about. Your final video will cut between you and the B-roll for a better viewer experience. For example, if you talk about how nice the kitchen is but you don't show the kitchen, viewers will get frustrated. I'll show you how to mix these videos together for the final cut.

CAMTASIA® VIDEO EDITOR

There are lots of good video editors out there. If you already know how to use an editor and you can mix B-roll clips, than you can skip this next part. If you don't have a video editor, I'll show you how to use Camtasia by Tech Smith. Camtasia is great for beginners and there are lots of tutorials on their website.

To edit video that you record on your phone, you will need to transfer the video to your computer where you have Camtasia installed. These video clips will be too large to text or email, so you will need to transfer them via the cloud, AirPlay, memory card, or a USB cord. If you are not sure how to do this, do a Google or YouTube search on how to transfer video with your specific phone to a PC or Mac. It's easy, but each device and option may be a little different, so I'll let you look it up. I've included video tutorials in our **Help** section of our website. We also teach this in our live class, Become the Community Go-to Agent. Don't let this software and video editing intimidate you. It's a lot easier than you think. Be patient and learn the tools of your trade, because video is a very important part of your real estate sales efforts. See the next page for a quick overview of the Camtasia video editor.

Download Camtasia
Buy Camtasia or try it for free

https://fxo.co/FdAx

COMMUNITY **GO-TO AGENT**

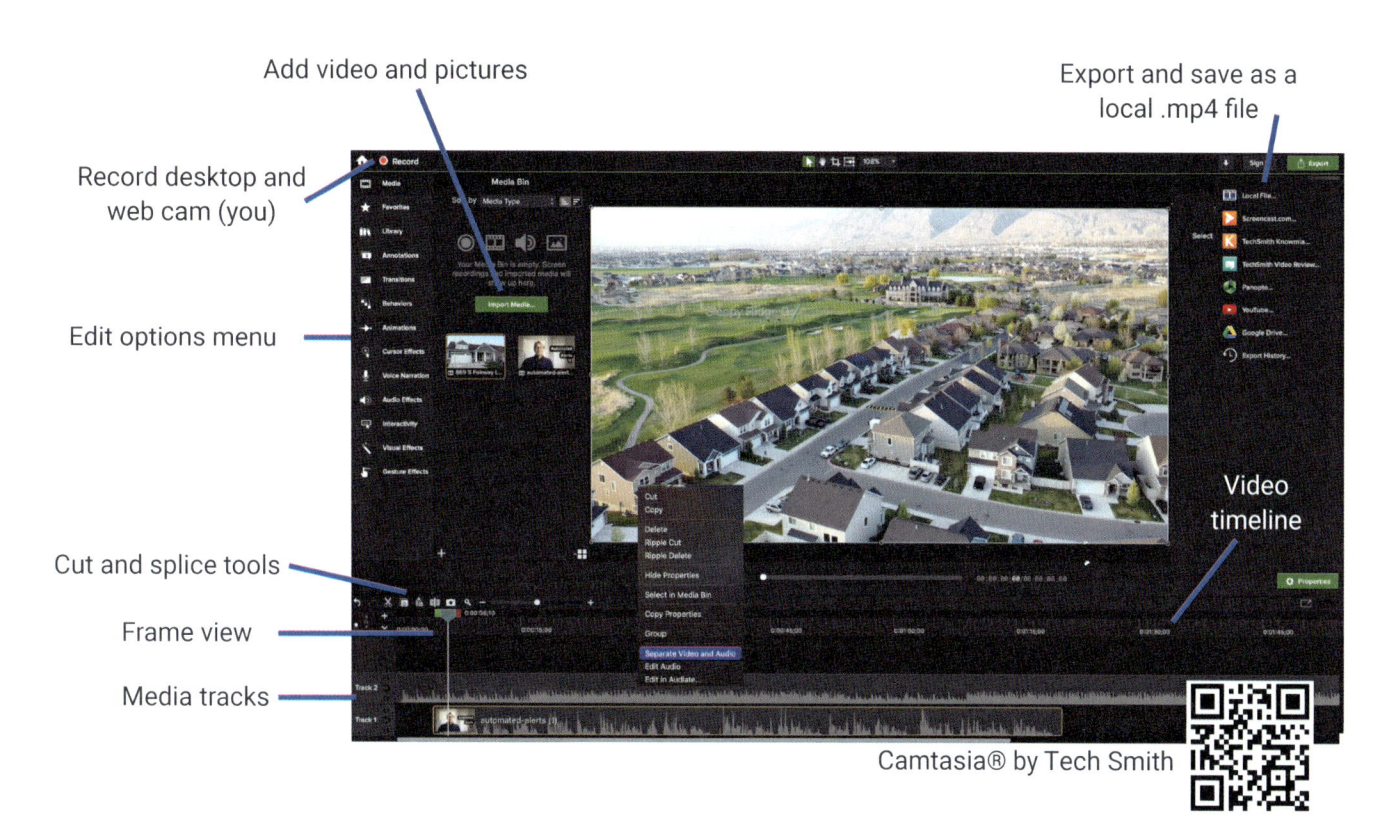

Screenshot of Camtasia video editing workspace with the following labels:
- Add video and pictures
- Record desktop and web cam (you)
- Edit options menu
- Cut and splice tools
- Frame view
- Media tracks
- Export and save as a local .mp4 file
- Video timeline

Camtasia® by Tech Smith

Camtasia is a relatively simple and intuitive program. The video editing workspace above provides a quick overview of the editing tools and options. Use the QR code on the upper right of this page to purchase Camtasia. Use the QR code below for Help video tutorials.

The first step is to import your video(s) from your phone. You can also import pictures, such as your head shot and logo. Drag the videos and pictures into the video timeline. Put the interview or main video on the bottom track. Place the B-roll and pictures on the top track(s). Everything added to the timeline will play in your video, so whatever is on the top track is what is seen. Place the videos or pictures where you want them to appear in your video. Use the cut and splice tools to remove any video you don't want. You can move video around anywhere you want in the timeline.

Right click a video track and select **Separate Video and Audio**. This will allow you to delete audio tracks from your B-roll so the only sound is from the main video.

You can experiment with the edit option tools to add annotations, transitions, and other affects. When you are done editing, export and save as a local .mp4 file. You can upload the .mp4 file to social media.

Help!
Video Tutorials
Watch a video on how to make a video :)

115

©2023 All rights reserved. Confidential and Proprietary. Intercap Lending, Inc.

8

**TIME
BLOCKING
POWER HOUR**

CHAPTER EIGHT
Time Blocking Power Hour

Time blocking is the discipline of designating a specific day and time to do a needed task, and blocking it off on your calendar so nothing can take its place. These tasks become intentional routines, with the understanding that making a daily effort over time is more significant than a big effort every now and then. Think of daily routines like exercise, intermittent fasting, or flossing your teeth, and how effective they are if you do them every day.

Your **Power Hour** will be one of the most important time blocks of your sales routine. In a single hour, you can capture new opportunities by identifying who needs your help based on where they are in the homeowner lifecycle. This is a very important distinction from a traditional sales call. Every call in the Captivate Program has a purpose of giving, not taking. When we call to ask for something, we're taking. When we know what someone needs and we offer to help, we're giving. Think of it like a service call instead of a sales call. You'll see what I mean when we review the call lists and what you have to offer.

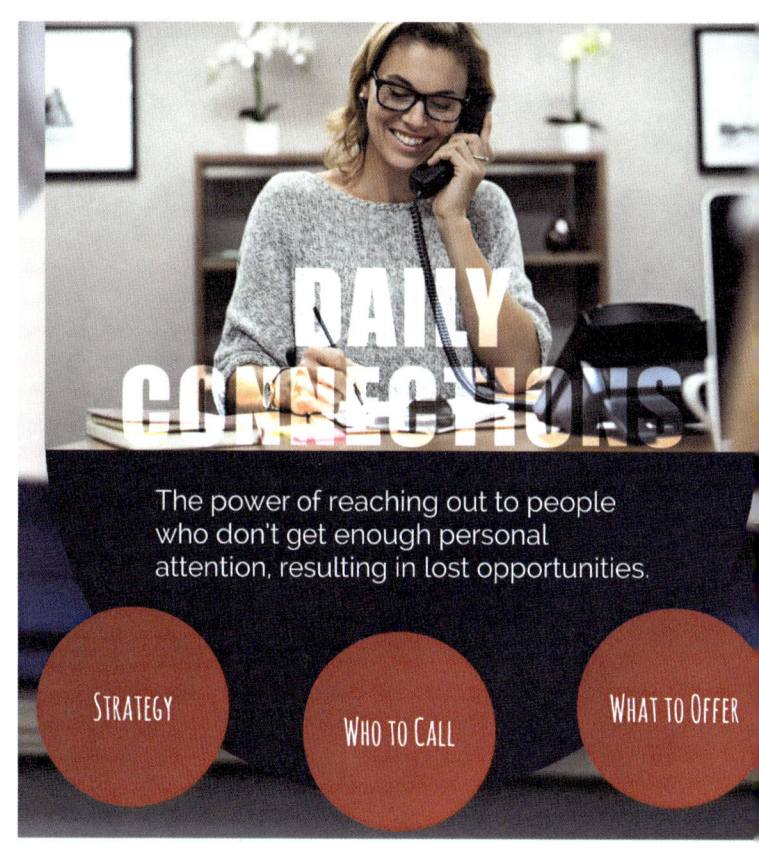

We call this power hour, **Captivate Daily Connections**. Its power is in the one-hour commitment, five days a week. The best time to commit to this power hour is in the morning around 10 to 11 am before the demands of the day take over. Some Captivate agents block this hour every weekday morning. Others take off a couple days during the week so they can attend their broker sales meeting and take a training class, and then add Saturday and Sunday to their weekly power hour calls. This also helps if some of the people you call are more available on the weekend. Whatever time block you decide for your power hour, make it consistent and stay committed. This is the most important daily commitment for business growth. A few more time blocking best practices include:

- Get dressed for the day and make your calls in an office, even if it's your home office. This power hour will be more productive if you treat it like an important workday task. You will also be ready to meet with clients as soon as you are done.

- If you decide to spend more than an hour making these calls, don't skip the next day. The consistent, daily effort is more powerful than a herculean but sporadic effort. It's alright to take personal days off without worrying about making them up.

- It's also alright to feel a little apprehensive about these calls the first few weeks. It's not alright, at least not for your business growth, to keep putting this off and never developing these calling skills. The longer you do this, the better you will be at making appointments over the phone.

We call this a **Daily Connection** because you are connecting people with the tools and resources they need to move forward with their real estate goals. Depending on the need, you may be connecting people with lenders, contractors, property managers, accountants, or other real estate-related professionals as you prepare your clients to buy and sell. You shouldn't simply refer your clients to these partners, at least not for the initial planning meetings. You should meet together to discuss how to support your clients as a team. You want to be your client's first point of contact when it comes to real estate. This is not about creating extra work for yourself, but added value. Learning about the other specialties in home ownership, and working closely with your partners makes you more valuable to your client, which will lead to more referrals.

The people you will connect with during this Power Hour are your sphere of influence (SOI). These include current clients, past clients, partners, community leaders, family, friends, neighbors, and all the people they refer. Your SOI will continue to grow as you help these people. The power hour goal is to keep your people moving through the homeowner lifecycle, with you and your partners as their trusted advisors.

In addition to these SOI calls, many agents also purchase leads, particularly in the beginning of their career. According to **Agent Legend** and a **State of Leads Survey** it conducted in 2021, most agents spend between $500 and $1,000 a month on leads, with about 10% of agents spending $10,000 or more per month[1]. Leads are the life blood of a growing business, so until you can generate enough leads from your SOI, purchased leads and lead advertising are a good way to supplement your lead pool. Response time is critical with these online lead sources, so you will want to contact these leads as soon as they come in. Once they are your clients, you can incorporate them into your daily power hour, converting them into raving fans and lifetime clients, thus becoming less dependent on these purchased leads.

The Daily Connections Strategy and Workflow
The **Daily Connection Workflow** starts with a phone call. The goal of the call is to make an appointment that hopefully leads to a new signed agreement. Once you have an agreement, you can create a plan to help your clients get ready to buy and sell.

> LEADS ARE THE LIFE BLOOD OF A GROWING BUSINESS

Daily Connections Strategy

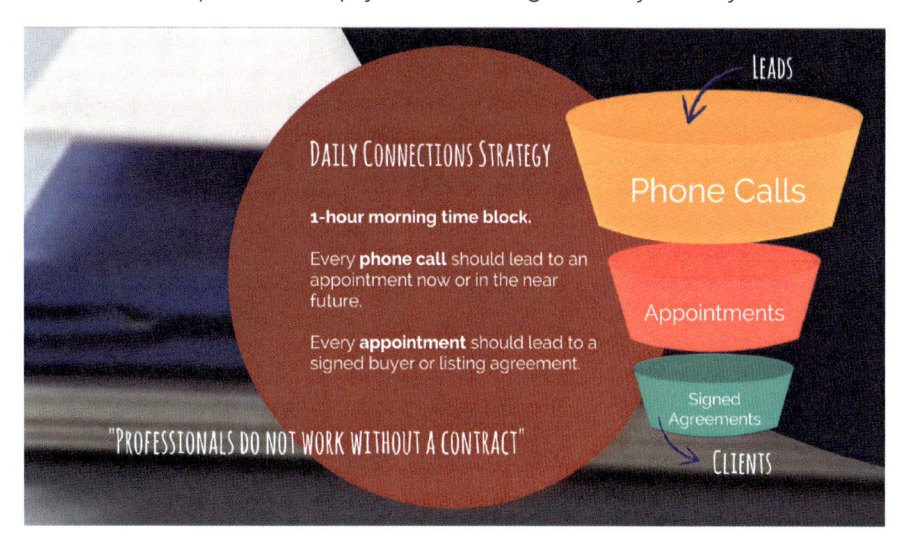

1-hour morning time block.

Every **phone call** should lead to an appointment now or in the near future.

Every **appointment** should lead to a signed buyer or listing agreement.

"Professionals do not work without a contract"

Leads → Phone Calls → Appointments → Signed Agreements → Clients

Each Captivate appointment is based on a client or partner need, identified by the following four calling groups.
1. House Shopping Without You
2. Waiting to Buy or Sell
3. Sphere of Influence (SOI)
4. Partners

The first two groups are current clients or opportunities that

---

[1] https://www.agentlegend.com/blog/resources/lead-conversion/how-much-do-most-real-estate-professionals-spend-on-lead-generation-you-might-be-surprised

TIME BLOCKING **POWER HOUR**

> **YOUR POWER HOUR IS A STEADY ROUTINE THAT CAN HAVE A SIGNIFICANT OUTCOME OVER TIME**

you don't want to lose. You will start your calls each day making sure everyone in these first two groups are taken care of. When you exhaust these call lists, you can move on to your third and fourth groups: SOI and Partners.

You only need to spend one hour a day on these calls. Whether you talk to two people or twenty in an hour, it doesn't matter. Each day after you make your hour worth of calls, mark where you left off and start again the next day. This is a steady routine, not an urgent, "I need to call until I get another deal" routine. Over time, service-based calls are more effective than sales-based calls. You can get the deals this way without desperate sales calls, but you need to learn how to get people to open up about their real estate goals and then help them plan.

GROUP 1 - HOUSE SHOPPING WITHOUT YOU
The **House Shopping Without You** group includes all your buyers until they go under contract. You never want a week to go by without giving home shoppers new properties to look at, otherwise they are likely "shopping without you." This is not a forget-me-not reminder call, it's a "I have home for you to look at" call. You are going to use your Captivating Buyers tools and techniques we discussed in chapter six, including traceable hot sheets, Insider Information, Distinctive Homes, and your buyer lead tracker on your website to help this group move forward with a purchase. Here is the recommended process with this House Shopping Without You group.

Pro Agent Website
This is what a buyer leader board looks like. It shows all your buyers and their activity on your agent website.

Visit www.proagentwebsites.com/intercap for more information

1. Check your buyer leader board on your website and identify anyone who hasn't visited homes with you over the last week. See how active your buyers are on your website based on the homes they viewed, and start with the most active buyers (see example to the left).

2. Every week, pick at least one home that fits the buyer's

criteria. Print out the MLS sheet and conduct your Insider Information. Start with the homes that your buyers looked at online, especially if they viewed the home several times. Your Insider Information may be a good reason to consider this home more seriously even if they didn't call you about it.

3. If you think it will help, find at least one more Distinctive Home to help the buyer consider properties outside their selected area or price range. This is especially important when inventory is low or your clients are struggling to find a home that has everything they want.

4. Here's an example of what you could say to these buyers, "I found a couple homes I think you are going to like. I also have some good Insider Information to share. I'll text you the homes. When would you like to go out this week to look at these homes and any others you may want to consider?"

5. If a client has already contacted you to see a home this week, that's great! There's no need to increase the frequency as long as a week doesn't go by without an opportunity to look at new homes. Keep up with the Insider Information and Distinctive Homes until they go under contract.

GROUP 2 - WAITING TO BUY OR SELL
The second group is **Waiting to Buy or Sell**. These are people you identified with specific next steps to buy or sell properties. This list could include those preparing for a future transaction, or those who asked you to contact them at a future date. Here are the steps for working with this group.

- Every time you talk or meet with someone about their real estate goals or wishes, which should happen often, you will add this information to your contact database (CMS). If there is an obvious next step, add this as a task reminder. It's important to treat conversations as an opportunity to make an appointment for next steps. If you do this consistently,

Pro Agent Website Discount Offer
www.proagentwebsites.com/Intercap

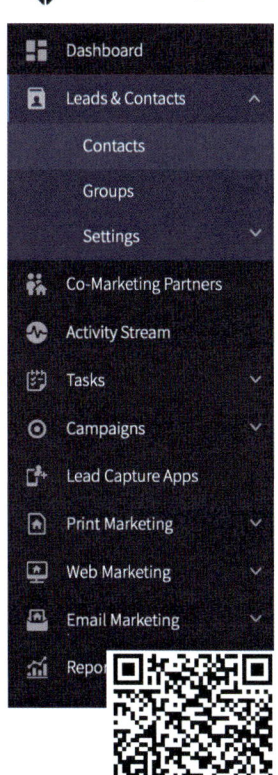

Sign up for Total Expert

TIME BLOCKING **POWER HOUR**

your CMS task list should have daily task reminders. These constitute your second Power Hour call list.

- When you are ready to call this group, check your database for your task or appointment reminders. If you don't have a contact database, get a free copy of Total Expert from your Intercap loan officer. You should be able to see all your task reminders on your dashboard. As long as you update these reminders regularly as people share their future goals, you should have plenty of daily reminders from past conversations.

GROUP 3 - SPHERE OF INFLUENCE (SOI)

The third call group is the rest of your **SOI**. The goal of this call list is to move opportunities into the first two call groups: Home Shopping Without You or Waiting to Buy and Sell. It's alright if they are still several months or years away from a real estate transaction. Your goal is to find out what they hope for and when you should start helping them prepare.

Captivate splits your SOI into three sub-categories: 1. **A-list,** 2. **High Equity,** and 3. **Alphabet List**. Your **A-list** consists of anyone who has sent you a referral over the past twelve months. You never want a month to go by without contacting the people in your A-list. The biggest difference with this call list is you are going to treat them to a lunch, coffee, or a pop-bye. They know what you want, so there's no need to ask. Just strengthen your relationship with this group by getting together once a month.

The next SOI list consists of all those that have a good amount of home equity, which is a good reason to make a move. You can find the people with high equity in your Homebot contacts. In **Homebot,** you can filter your contacts by the amount of home equity they have and how often they look at their home digest. Start with the homeowners that are most engaged with their monthly digest. Here is a suggested script for calling someone with a lot of home equity.

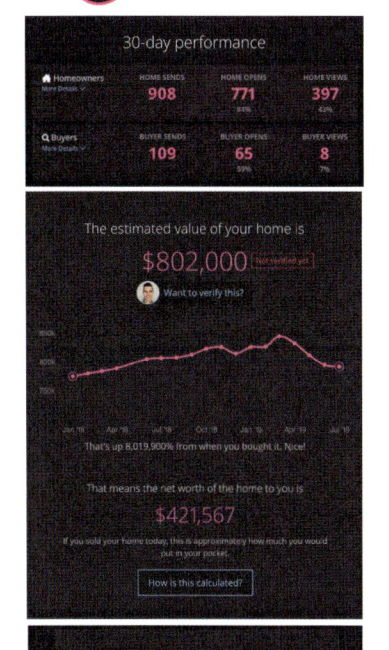

"I was looking at your Home Equity Digest I sent you this month and I noticed you have been checking on it too. How do you feel about this information? Has it been helpful?" Let the conversation develop naturally. If it makes sense, say, "I noticed you have an estimated [dollar amount] of home equity. Have you thought about doing something with your equity?" Let the homeowner take the lead on their thoughts before trying to sell them on their options.

If the homeowner sounds confused or isn't sure, say something like this, "Home equity gives homeowners a lot of options. You could move to a new home with less impact on your monthly mortgage, you could refinance to lower your monthly costs, you could take out cash, pay off your home and debt more quickly, or you could buy a second home or investment property. Do any of these options sound interesting? Many people don't realize the potential of leveraging their home equity to buy property or get in a better financial position."

The appointments that come from these options will need to include your lender partner so the three of you can discuss financial specifics and next steps. We'll talk about possible appointments after we cover these call lists.

Once you've exhausted this **High Equity SOI** list, you can work on the rest of your **SOI by Alphabet**. Call last names that start with A in week one, B's in week two and so forth. There are 26 letters in the alphabet and 52 weeks in a year. That means you should reach every person in your SOI at least twice a year. You are not calling to sell, but to get people to share with you what they might be considering in real estate, now or in the future. The goal is to get them talking about what they have thought about doing and suggest that you can help them plan for this next step.

TIME BLOCKING **POWER HOUR**

As I've said from the start, you shouldn't call without something to offer, based on what your clients want. The people in the first group, **Home Shopping Without You**, want to buy a home, so you should offer them at least one new home to look at every week with some helpful Insider Information. The people in your second group, **Waiting to Buy or Sell**, already let you know what they wanted and you added this to your task list. You are simply following up based on your notes and reminders. Your **SOI A-list** gets a monthly reminder that you appreciate them. Your SOI with high equity have some financial options worth exploring, and you can track their interest and equity in Homebot to determine their interest. The rest of your SOI likely has some thoughts about what they would like to do at some point in the future, and the purpose of your call is to get them to open up about their wish list and see how you and your partners can help.

It may be hard to get the conversation started with someone who hasn't shared with you what help they may need when it comes to a future real estate transaction, so I included recommendations on how to get them to open up.

RENTERS IN YOUR MARKET WILL WANT YOUR **PATHWAY TO QUALIFICATION** PLAN

Calling Renters

If you are speaking with a renter, say something like this: "We've got this new program called the **Pathway to Qualification** to help renters buy their first home by the time their lease is up or whenever it makes sense. How would you like a plan to buy your own place?" Listen to their response and let the renter share their thoughts. You can also add, "Our Pathway to Qualification program tells you exactly how close you are to buying and what you need to get ready. We also give you a Buy vs Rent report, an equity projection based on where you want to buy, and information about no down payment options. It's a plan to help you buy in the future when it makes sense for you. When can you meet to get started?"

HOME EQUITY IS THE #1 REASON HOMEOWNERS BUY AGAIN

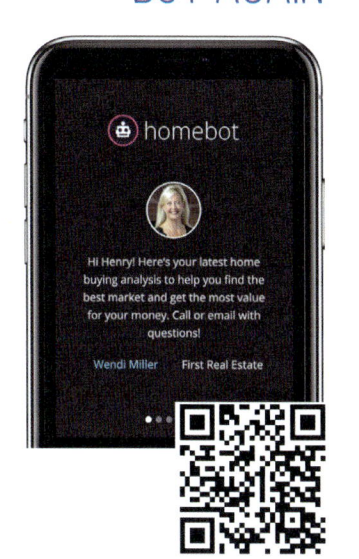

Calling Homeowners

If you are speaking to a homeowner, say something like this: "I invested in this new system so my clients and friends can track their home value. It creates a Home Equity Statement that shows your estimated home's value and equity every month. It's odd that we get monthly investment and bank statements, but we don't get a statement on our most valuable asset, our homes! I'm really excited to share this with you."

You will want to create a Homebot digest for homeowners as you speak with them. Fill out all the information about their home and confirm their email address while on the phone. Open the digest and say, "Ok, I'm going to send this to you right now. Wow, It shows you have an estimated [dollar amount] in home equity. Does that sound about right? Take a look at what I just sent you and tell me what you think." Direct the conversation to their options for leveraging this equity and ask, "Have you thought about doing something with your equity, like moving up or investing in another property?"

Power Hour Calls Should Lead to Appointments

The Power Hour strategy is to turn your calls into appointments. You want to give clients just enough information to get them to meet with you in person or over a video conference call so you can make a plan. You may need your lender or other partners with you at these appointments.

The purpose of your appointments is to determine what your clients should do to prepare to buy or sell, even if it takes several months. You and your partners' ability to help clients plan their next move is what makes you more valuable as a real estate consultant. This approach also gives you the opportunity to help anyone you speak with. If you are only looking for those who are ready to buy or sell right now, you will potentially annoy about 95% of the people you reach out to. Now you can offer to help at any stage of the homeowner lifecycle.

CAPTIVATE
7 CUSTOMER APPOINTMENTS

Let's review these appointments in more detail. Your appointments should be based on a **Homeowner Program** that supports a **Plan** with set of **Action Items**. In Captivate, we call this the **PPA approach**. As a Captivate real estate consultant, you now have seven appointment options to help clients prepare to buy and sell, no matter where they are in the homeowner lifecycle. This is how you create new clients and opportunities every day.

1. Listing Appointment
2. Showing Appointment
3. First-time Buyer Appointment
4. Home Transition Appointment
5. Investor Appointment
6. Downsizer Appointment
7. Relocator Appointment

PROGRAM	PLAN(S)	ACTION ITEMS
1. Home Seller Prep Program **Audience:** Homeowners **Offer:** Help owners maximize their net gain and sell just in time.	• $20k Listing Service • Home Staging Plan • Grand Open House Plan • Home Transition Plan	• Listing Report/True Value • Home preparation • Pictures, drone, and Matterport • MLS listing, 5 Ads, and landing pages • Grand Open House • Before and after video
2. Home Shopping Program **Audience:** Home buyers **Offer:** Help buyers find the right home using today's technology, Insider Information, and Distinctive Homes.	• Weekly Home Shopping Plan • Under Contract Plan • Home Transition Plan	• Loan Approval Guarantee • Listing alerts and Homebuyer App • Insider Information • Distinctive Homes • Loan Status Updates

CAPTIVATE
7 CUSTOMER APPOINTMENTS

PROGRAM	PLAN(S)	ACTION ITEMS
3. First-time Buyer Program Audience: Renters Offer: Help renters with a plan to purchase a home by the time their lease is up or within a year.	• Pathway to Qualification Plan • House Hacking Plan • Captivate Retirement Plan • Home Transition Plan (from a rental)	• Meet with lender and fill out **P2Q Form** to determine how close the buyer is to qualifying for a mortgage • Set goals for credit, down payment, and DTI • Prepare **Buy vs Rent Report** • Create budget and consider **House Hacking** options to subsidize mortgage • Create a **Retirement Plan** using rental properties
4. Home Transition Program Audience: Homeowners that want to move in the area Offer: Help owner with a plan to transition to a new home considering their budget and financial goals.	• Home Transition Plan • Budget and Finance Plan • Home Prep Plan	• Time the sale and purchase to avoid two mortgages or no place to live • Get house ready to sell (Captivate Listing Service) • Meet with lender and accountant to review equity, debt, and budget considerations • Meet with lender to discuss the possibility of renting current property
5. Investor Program Audience: Property investors interested in long or short-term rentals, second homes, and vacation properties Offer: Help investors explore loan options, locations, and other details.	• First Rental Property Plan • Short-term Rental Plan • Buy and Flip Plan • Second Home or Vacation Home Plan	• Read **Rental Property Investing** by Brandon Carter • Subscribe to **Bigger Pockets** • Meet with lender to discuss budget, CAP rates, investor loans, and **Equity Forecasting** • Meet with lender to discuss leveraging home equity to purchase a rental property • Get listing alerts based on preferred location, property type, and budget • Provide a list of recommended service providers and contractors

CAPTIVATE
7 CUSTOMER APPOINTMENTS

PROGRAM	PLAN(S)	ACTION ITEMS
6. Downsizer Program **Audience:** Homeowners planning for retirement and/or empty-nesters **Offer:** Help owners downsize for retirement	• Home Transition Plan • Budget and Finance Plan • Home Prep Plan (Similar planning as **Home Transition**, but geared to buyers who have or will have a fixed income)	Same as the Home Transition Planning with the following additional considerations with assistance from CPA and lender. • Reverse Mortgage options • Use equity from sale to purchase retirement home and rental properties • Options for condos and 55+ communities
7. Relocator Program **Audience:** Homeowners planning to move out of the area Offer: Help owners plan their move out of the state or area	• Home Transition Plan • Home Prep Plan • Pre-approval Plan	• Get house ready to sell (Captivate Listing Service) • Contact referral agent in new location to discuss Transition Plan • Meet with lender to discuss mortgage options and get client pre-approved before they move to avoid delays (Intercap loan officers are licensed in most states)

Just about everyone over the age of 25 has an aspiration for their next step in real estate. Your ability to get them to share their ideas with you and say, "**We have a program for that**," will allow you to pull them into your **Captivate Homeowner Lifecycle** so you can help them accomplish their real estate goals with a good plan. You don't have to help everyone. You can still be picky about who you help so you don't waste time on those who are not serious about moving forward.

You will need your strategic partners, like lenders and contractors, to help with your appointments and to deliver your services. These make up your support team. Your fourth Power Hour group are partners. Your goal is to establish your partner relationships by meeting with them regularly and collaborating on how you can help each other. You have as much to offer your partners as they have to offer you, as you both work together to help your shared clients.

STRATEGIC PARTNERS

Strategic Partners are those who are critical to your core offerings, like your broker, coordinators, mortgage lender, and escrow officer.

YOU AND YOUR PARTNERS CAN BE THE BEST REAL ESTATE TEAM IN YOUR MARKET

4. PARTNER GROUP

Your Partner group includes **Strategic Partners** and **Support Partners**. Strategic Partners are those who are critical to your core offerings. These should include your broker, coordinators, mortgage lender, escrow officer, home warranty representative, stager, photographer, home power washer, deep cleaner, and a lawn care professional. Depending on your niche farm focus, you may also have a property manager, real estate lawyer, CPA, or other specialists. Support partners will include a variety of home service providers, contractors, insurance agents, and inspectors.

These partner relationships are about quality, not quantity. This isn't a quid-pro-quo exchange, and you shouldn't try to partner with every professional hoping to get more referrals or hand-outs. If you think of these people as business partners rather than affiliates or referral partners, you can build strategic business relationships with shared goals and integrated workflows. Be picky about your partners, and be a good partner to them.

When you meet, you should discuss how you can work better together in the best interest of your shared clients. Discuss the Captivate Appointments and Programs, and how your partner services can integrate with your services. Get them to commit to this partnership, and if they won't, find someone who will.

You should meet regularly to collaborate about co-marketing opportunities, integrated workflows, lessons learned, and business goals. Both businesses should flourish because the overall support to the client is better when you work together.

Now is the time to create a real estate consulting offering where you are a Master Connector of all things real estate. Buyers, sellers, contractors, partners, and community leaders all need you as much as you need them, and you are in the best position to bring this packaged real estate consulting offering to your shared clients.

CAP88 CHALLENGE

This Power Hour routine, with all of the appointment opportunities, is going to take some time to master. To make this easier, we have developed a **Cap88 Challenge**. This is an 88-day Captivate accountability challenge to get your technology setup, define your annual goals, and start your Daily Connections with some helpful support. The Cap88 Tracker provides 12-weeks of tracking your Power Hour calls and appointments. You can also join Cap88 Coaching Groups that work together to master all that Captivate has to offer.

www.intercaplending.com/cap88

9

THE MORNING ROUTINE

CHAPTER NINE
The Morning Routine

When I teach this class in person, I ask participants, "Who here has a morning routine?" About 20% raise their hand. This means 20% have a morning routine they intentionally follow. The rest still have a routine, but perhaps not so intentional. We are, by nature, creatures of habit. Think about what you do each morning and you probably follow a similar routine. Growth happens when we consider our habits and decide to make intentional changes that help us reach new goals. Just like the Power Hour we discussed in the last chapter, small intentional routines can have a significant impact over time.

I recently met a 22 year old track athlete from one of the local universities. I asked her how much she ran to keep in shape for her track meets. My jaw dropped when she told me 45 miles a week. That's nearly the distance of two marathons every week. She's been running five to eight miles a day since junior high. It's who she is. We all have the same amount of time each day. The question is, how will we use that time to accomplish our goals?

For many of us, our day is already packed full of commitments. We've committed time for work, family, entertainment, church, sports, and hobbies. My son's soccer coach has a full-time job, three young kids, and loves to camp and travel. Like her, most of us have a full life, and it can be hard to dedicate time to something new. Yet many of us have this nagging feeling that we should do more, or do better.

The early morning is that special time of the day that we can ultimately control what we do, at least if we get up before other demands pull us away. It can also set the stage for how we deal with our daily demands. A good morning routine can help you face the day a little stronger physically, mentally, and emotionally. An intentional morning routine may be that missing piece that helps you accomplish your goals in all areas of your life, without having to make sweeping changes to your daily commitments.

How Long is a Good Morning Routine?

I've experimented with different lengths of time and morning activities and settled into a ninety-minute routine that works for me. Your routine may be longer or shorter, and involve different activities than mine. I've adapted my morning routine several times over the years as I've learned about things like meditation and intermittent fasting. What you do and the amount of time you spend should fit your values and lifestyle. This is personal time to charge your mental, physical, and emotional batteries so you can hit the ground running each day.

The amount of time you allocate to your morning routine will determine how early you need to get up. You will want to complete your morning routine before your daily commitments start, and without causing undue stress to your schedule and commitments. Here is what I try to do each weekday morning:

Make my Bed - 5 minutes

The first thing I do to start with a win is to make my bed. This may sound silly, but it's an important part of my morning routine. My inspiration for this came from the book, **Make Your Bed**, by Admiral William H. McRaven. Making your bed is a good way to keep from getting back in bed and creates a tangible win first thing in the morning. One thing I **don't do** first thing in the morning is check my phone.

Exercise - 30 minutes

After laying down all night, it's important to get the blood pumping and your body back in motion. According to several studies, a daily morning exercise can help:
- Boost my energy throughout the day
- Improve my focus and cognition
- Put me in a better mood
- Lower my risk of health problems like diabetes
- Get a better night's sleep

Thirty minutes of a high-intensity aerobic and strength workout,

TIME **MORNING ROUTINE**

with some flexibility, warm-up, and cool-down exercises helps me stay healthy and in shape. I used to go to the gym, but during Covid I discovered an online exercise training site that offers a variety of cardio, HIIT, PLYO, and other exercise programs that I can do from home. This has allowed me to bring my entire morning routine down to 90-minutes, and it gives me more workout options than I had when I went to the gym each day. If you want to try this online workout, I included a free trial and discount option to the left.

Get a Beachbody.com discount or free trial

Shower and Dress - 15 minutes

During the last minute of my shower, I turn the water as cold as I can stand it. This helps stimulate my vagus nerve, which many doctors believe has physical and mental benefits such as improving mood and the ability to manage stress. I notice an immediate difference in my energy and alertness as a natural post work-out energy boost.

One-page Goal Sheet

As I get dressed, I read my one-page goal sheet out loud. In the Cap88 Coaching Program, we help agents setup their **12-month Growth Plan** with measurable goals, routines, and milestones, all written on a one-page goal sheet. I recommend hanging this sheet on the bathroom mirror or next to your closet so you can read it each morning as you get dressed. This routine will imprint these goals in your mind and help you remember what you want to accomplish. The effect this has on accomplishing goals is hard to quantify. It's almost supernatural.

Cap88 and the One-page Goal Sheet

Meditate - 10 to 15 minutes

The ability to manage fears, stress, anxiety, and negativity is especially important for business owners, entrepreneurs, and self-employed workers like real estate agents. It's difficult to take on the responsibilities of managing a business and

MINDFULNESS AND KINDNESS MAKE FOR A HAPPIER LIFE

believing you can keep things running each day without the safety net of a salary. About 10 years ago, I read a book by Shirzad Chamine called **Positive Intelligence**. His scientific approach to positivity as a measurable quotient intrigued me. It was the first time I bought into the idea of meditation. Since then, it has transformed how I see myself, others, and the challenges I face each day. I wish I had read this book when I was a teenager! I try to listen to Shirzad's book at least once a year. It's a great read if you need some context to why meditation and mindfulness are helpful.

There are also two excellent meditation phone apps I use to help with simple meditative exercises each morning, which I can finish in under 15 minutes: Calm and Headspace. They are definitely worth the small investment, and I provided a discount link to Headspace on the left margin.

20-minutes of Service
I'm still working on this one, but I discovered a morning activity that has already been a game changer for my relationships. My task is to do something simple, kind, and unexpected for someone each morning. The unexpected part is what makes this small act of kindness so impactful. Here are some of the things I have done in 20-mintues or less. This list continues to grow.

- Write and mail a letter to a friend or relative I haven't spoken to in a while. Not an email or text, an actual letter.
- Put a nice note in your child's backpack or lunch that they won't find until they get to school.
- Send flowers to your mother when it's not a holiday.
- Think of someone who helped you this week and send them a thank you card.
- Clean a room, make a bed, do the dishes, clean a toilet, or anything that you might not do regularly because someone else does it for you.
- Leave a favorite drink in your spouse's car, or someone that you live with.

TIME **MORNING ROUTINE**

- Tell your teenage children how nice they look and how amazing they are before they leave to school (no matter how they dress or how grumpy they act).
- If your kids take the bus to school, drive them one day.
- Send your child's teacher a thank you card.
- Take the time to learn the names of your co-workers' family.
- Make breakfast for someone who's running late.

Bedtime Routine

I also have a few things I do most nights to make sure my morning routine is more effective. I guess you could call this my bedtime routine. Yes, even adults can use a bedtime routine.

- The amount of sleep I get is very important to my physical and mental health. According to many reputable sources, an adult needs seven or more hours of sleep. I start my morning routine at 6:30 am on weekdays, so I try to get to bed by 10 pm.

- I try to avoid screen time an hour before I want to go to sleep. I've personally noticed a difference in my time to fall asleep and my quality of sleep.

- When I hit my late 40's, I started having stomach issues and I wouldn't sleep well. After lots of research and some trial and error, I finally decided not to eat between 7pm and 11am. There's too much information on this topic to cover here, and I am not a doctor or nutritionist, but this intermittent fasting has made a world of difference for my sleep, stomach issues, and my morning routine. It may be something to look into. I still drink water during this time, so it's not a true fast.

If you don't have your own morning routine, I highly suggest you create one that nurtures and challenges you. Starting the day

THE NEXT DAY IS EASIER WITH A GOOD NIGHT'S REST

with a routine focused on your physical, mental, and emotional well-being can set you up for a more successful day, ready to take on the challenges you can't always control.

I remember times I've been lost, distracted, anxious, worried, tired, frustrated, and down right negative. Times where I doubted myself, believing that my wins were dumb luck, and my losses deserved. Times when I was arrogant and thought I had everything figured out. It wasn't until my morning routine that I began to experience some balance, peace, acceptance, and some needed truth. Here is some of that truth I continue to learn each morning as I prepare for the day.

- I am lucky and very blessed, and it's alright to be lucky. I don't have to know everything or be entirely responsible for my successes or failures. And neither does anyone else.

- It's alright to fail. The world doesn't end and the sun keeps rising.

- Thinking of others first has a bigger return than putting myself first. But it has to be genuine.

- I have to remind myself daily to get out of my own way.

- If I constantly remind myself what I want to accomplish, and I'm intentional about what I can do to accomplish it, remarkable things happen.

- Taking care of my mind and my body will enable me to do hard things, and I want to do hard things.

Many of the agents I coach through the Captivate Program initially get overwhelmed. It will seem like a lot of work, and at first, it is. You must believe in yourself and commit to doing hard things if you want to make a difference. The way you spend your morning will help you prepare mentally, physically,

IT'S ALRIGHT FOR THINGS TO BE HARD

IT'S ALRIGHT TO FAIL

IT'S ALRIGHT TO GET HELP

IT'S NOT ALRIGHT TO STOP TRYING

THE **CAPTIVATE TOOLS & ROUTINES**

and emotionally for the wonderful, yet tough things you face each day. Remarkably, as you get stronger, this work will no longer seem that hard. Your business success will come when your competition still complains that these things are too hard. Your personal success will come when you don't need to measure up to anyone.

THE CAPTIVATE TOOLS AND ROUTINES

The Captivate Program is easier to follow than you think, with a tremendous upside. The following table outlines the recommended Captivate Tools, and the next page shows the recommended Captivate Routines. Get the Cap88 Tracker and track these routines for 88 days until they become habits.

RECOMMENDED REAL ESTATE TOOLS AND TECHNOLOGIES

Contact Management Database	Total Expert
<ul><li>Manage contacts using groups, notes, and reminders</li><li>Create Single Property Websites and open house registrations</li><li>Create and share branded flyers</li></ul>	www.intercaplending.com/total-expert
Buyer Lead Management and Agent Website	**Pro Agent Website & The Homebuyer App**
<ul><li>Manage buyers with SMS hot sheets and lead tracking</li><li>Add farm listings to your Facebook Group</li><li>Create farm landing pages</li><li>Give your buyers the Homebuyer App with GPS Home Searches</li></ul>	www.proagentwebsites.com/intercap www.intercaplending.com/homebuyer
Home Value and Equity Statement	**Homebot**
<ul><li>Send monthly home value equity statements to homeowners</li><li>Send a monthly buyer digest to buyers</li></ul>	www.intercaplending.com/homebot
Captivate Listing Services	**PowerPoint, Tablet, and Leave Behinds**
<ul><li>$20k Listing Presentation slide deck</li><li>Branded home shopping bag and folder</li><li>Grand Open House signage</li></ul>	www.intercaplending.com/product-category/captivate/

THE **CAPTIVATE TOOLS & ROUTINES**

RECOMMENDED REAL ESTATE ROUTINES

CAPTIVATE DAILY ROUTINES	Description
Morning Routine	Prepare for each day mentally, physically, and emotionally (see chapter 9).
Power Hour	1-hour prospecting, 4 call lists, 7 appointment opportunities (see chapter 8)
Post new homes for sale and rent on your Farm Facebook Group	Add new listings, FSBOs, and rentals on your Facebook group. Text FSBO and property managers (see chapter 4)
CAPTIVATE WEEKLY ROUTINES	**Description**
Create Search Landing Pages	1x farm search landing page on your agent website (see chapter 4)
Attend Broker Sales Meetings	Pass out open house flyers to agents and invite them to your open house
Set Power Hour appointment goals	Use Cap88 Tracker to set weekly appointment goals (see chapter 9)
Attend Coaching Session or Training Class	Attend a weekly coaching or training class to improve your skills and knowledge
CAPTIVATE MONTHLY ROUTINES	**Description**
Host Client Dinner Party	A dinner celebration for all your clients who closed since the last dinner party, and anyone who referred them (see chapter 6)
Create Farm/Community Video, Custom Landing Page or Blog	1x farm community video and landing page posted to social media and linked to your agent website (see chapter 7)
Attend a City Council, Chamber of Commerce, and/or Realtor Association Meeting	Learn about what's going on in your farm and real estate market by attending these monthly meetings.
CAPTIVATE ANNUAL ROUTINES	**Description**
Make Annual Goals	Write 12-month goals on one-page goal sheet (Cap88 Challenge)
Take a Guiltless Vacation	Plan and take a non-working vacation (Cap88 Challenge)

THE **CAP88 CHALLENGE**

Get the Cap88 Tracker and take the 88-day challenge to help turn these ideas into an actionable growth plan. The Cap88 Tracker helps you:

- Create your annual goals on a one-page goal sheet that you will read each morning
- Get your technology setup and the key things these tools are used for
- Track 12-weeks of your Power Hour

Get the Cap88 Tracker at www.intercaplending.com/cap88

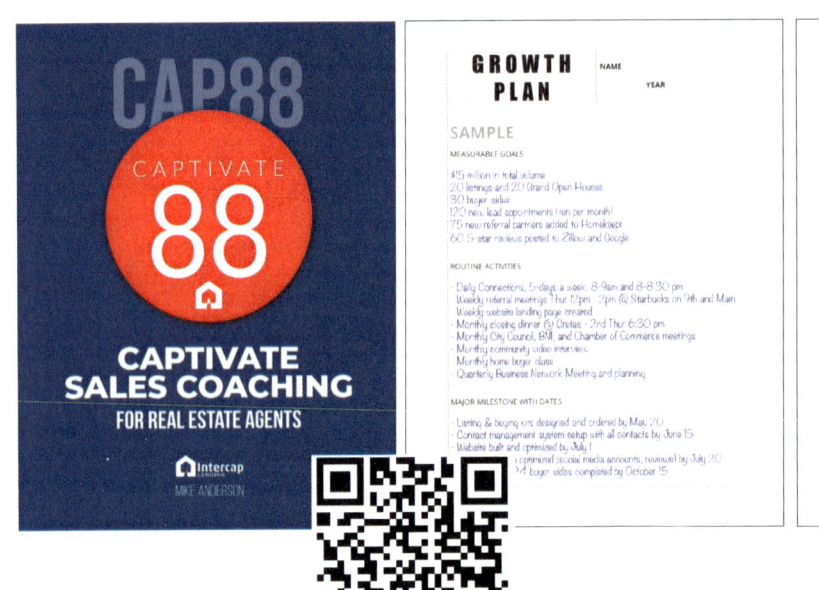

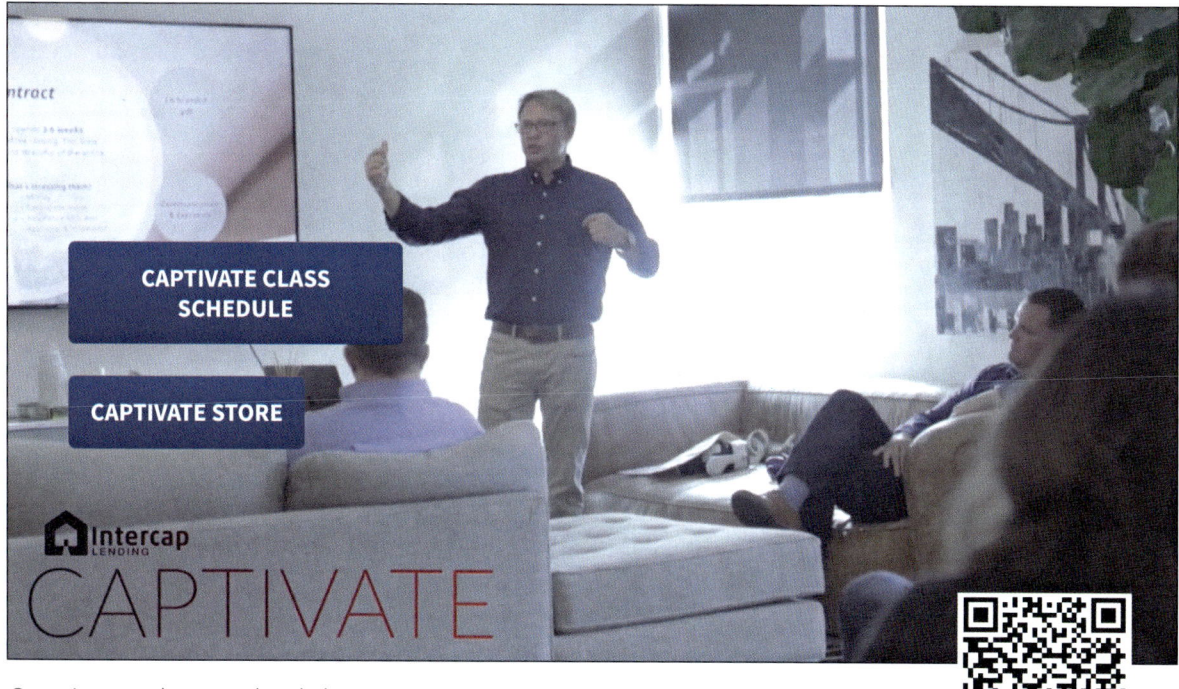

Captivate class schedules, training videos, and access to other Captivate resources can be found at www.intercaplending.com/

Live streamed classes, video examples, and other resources can be found at www.facebook.com/captivatesalescoaching